Building a Culture of Support

STRATEGIES FOR SCHOOL LEADERS

PJ Caposey

Eye On Education
6 Depot Way West, Suite 106
Larchmont, NY 10538
(914) 833–0551
(914) 833–0761 fax
www.eyeoneducation.com

Library of Congress Cataloging-in-Publication Data

Caposey, P. J.
Building a culture of support : strategies for school leaders / PJ Caposey.
    pages cm
    ISBN 978-1-59667-227-7
1. School management and organization--United States.   2. School
environment—United States.   3. Educational leadership—United
States. I. Title.
    LB2805.C2665 2012
    371.200973--dc23

                                                                    2012028207

10 9 8 7 6 5 4 3 2 1

Sponsoring Editor: Robert Sickles
Production Editor: Lauren Beebe
Copyeditor: Laurie Lieb
Designer and Compositor: Dan Kantor
Cover Designer: Dave Strauss, 3FoldDesign

Also Available from Eye On Education

What Great Principals Do *Differently*:
18 Things That Matter Most
(Second Edition)
Todd Whitaker

The Principal's Guide to the First 100 Days of the School Year:
Creating Instructional Momentum
Shawn Joseph

The Learning Leader:
Reflecting, Modeling, and Sharing
Jacqueline E. Jacobs, Kevin L. O'Gorman

Lead On!
Motivational Lessons for School Leaders
Pete Hall

The Fearless School Leader:
Making the Right Decisions
Cynthia McCabe

Communicate and Collaborate:
The School Leader's Guide to Effective Communication
Shelly Arneson

Leading School Change:
9 Strategies to Bring Everybody On Board
Todd Whitaker

Creating School Cultures That Embrace Learning:
What Successful Leaders Do
Tony Thacker, John S. Bell, & Franklin P. Schargel

Motivating and Inspiring Teachers:
The Educational Leader's Guide for Building Staff Moral
(Second Edition)
Todd Whitaker, Beth Whitaker, & Dale Lumpa

Creating School Cultures That Embrace Learning:
What Successful Leaders Do
Tony Thacker, John S. Bell, & Franklin P. Schargel

The Principalship from A to Z
Ronald Williamson & Barbara R. Blackburn

This book is dedicated to my family. I cannot explain how proud it makes me to wake up every day to be be Jacquie's husband and Jameson and Jackson's dad. This book is for you in hopes that it creates some positive change that impacts your lives as a teacher and students.

ACKNOWLEDGMENTS

Books do not write themselves. Trying to work through a project such as this as a husband, father, principal, and doctoral student has been challenging. This project would simply not have reached completion without the support and understanding of my wife, Jacquie. The routine of tucking our sons into bed and heading back to the office to grind through a few more pages never wore on her spirit or resolve, although it did on mine at times. I thank you and the boys (our sons Jameson and Jackson) for everything. I hope you can be as proud of this book as I am of you. I also want to thank both my and Jacquie's parents and siblings. They lost out on some time with me (I am sure they can get over that) but also with the kids as I was bunkered down on the weekends quite a bit more than usual. Your sacrifices did not go unnoticed and neither did the support and confidence you have given me over the years.

A philosophy of education is not something created in a vacuum. My career and educational beliefs have been influenced by everyone that I have had the pleasure of working alongside. A few noteworthy and giving educators and one organization have had a profound impact on my career and upon me personally. I would be remiss if I did not mention them by name.

♦ I would first like to acknowledge everyone who took a chance in hiring me. In hindsight it took courage for each of you to hire a young, inexperienced educator. Without each of you putting confidence in me, I would not be where I am today. Thank you, Dr. William Harris, Dr. Richard Jancek, and Dr. William Mattingly.

♦ The Golden Apple Foundation in Chicago, Illinois, is an underappreciated organization that provides top high school seniors with support, both professionally and financially, throughout their college careers, in return for service at need-based schools. This organization completely expanded my horizons, introduced me to diversity, and convinced me that working with at-risk youth is the greatest reward any educator can receive.

♦ Dr. Sandra Watkins of Western Illinois University is largely the reason that I am writing this book. Dr. Watkins cued me in to the possibilities that exist for passionate educators who are willing to work to spread their messages and accomplish their dreams.

♦ Dr. Gary Fields is a retired superintendent who works as a consultant in northwest Illinois. Dr. Fields has served as a consultant in two schools I have worked in and has had a profound impact on me professionally. Dr. Fields was the first person to explain to me the *why* that exists in education instead of just beating me over the head with the *what*.

♦ Dr. Richard Jancek has been a big brother to me throughout my administrative career. I learned much about the world of administration under Dr. J's tutelage, and nobody has provided my career with as much support as he. Dr. J has been there for my highest highs and lowest lows as an administrator and has always helped me keep things in perspective. Without his influence it would have been impossible for me to be a high school principal at the age of 28.

♦ Mr. Thomas Mahoney is my boss—and quite possibly the smartest person I know. Nobody has come close to influencing my professional life more than Tom. He has guided me through some of the most complex issues of my career and has also helped to shape and refine many of my beliefs and philosophies. Many of the views articulated throughout this book have been discussed and refined through administrative meetings and conversations over the past two years. I cannot imagine working for anybody who would be more supportive of my professional growth and personal ambitions.

I also need and want to acknowledge my colleagues in Oregon Community Unit School District 220. I have the privilege of working with an extremely capable and professional group of faculty and staff. If each of them has gained one-tenth as much from our experiences together as I have, they will have grown immensely. Thank you.

Adam Albrecht	Barry Barton	Colleen Beierle
John Bothe	Mike Boyer	Cheryl Bunton
Kip Crandall	Shannon Cremeens	Cole Davidson
Justin Ebert	Andy Eckardt	Shawn Gadow
Mark Gale	John Geeves	John Gonzales
Skip Gooch	Janet Greenwood	Mary Jo Griffin
Tracy Harvey	Missy Heisner	Phyllis Heuerman
Curt Howard	Lynn Kaufman	Darren Knuth
Adam Larsen	Danyel Larsen	Mitch Lauer
Mike Lawton	Glen Majewski	Mary Malloch
Megan Martin	Brenda McCaskey	Erin McMaster
Dy Mowry	Andrew Nelson	Mark Nerhkorn
Bruce Obendorf	Jan Pattat	Kim Radostits
Nick Schneiderman	Terry Schuster	Ken Scott
Aaron Sitze	Amy Smith	Ed Smith
Marilyn Spangler	Jim Spratt	Lori Spratt
Alice Starkey	Ann Tilton	Peg Trampel
Jim Turffs	Mary Verdun	Quinn Virgil
Sara Werckle	Bryan Wills	Phil Yordy
Frank Zelek	John Zuber	

ABOUT THE AUTHOR

PJ Caposey's educational career began in high school when he received the Golden Apple Scholarship, which supports students pursuing their dream to teach by providing financial aid and training in return for a commitment to teach in a needs-based area. Mr. Caposey did just that after completing his studies at Eastern Illinois University by teaching at Percy Lavon Julian High School in Chicago.

After completing his administrative certification at National Louis University, Mr. Caposey served as an Assistant Principal in Rockford Public Schools before becoming the principal of Oregon High School at the age of 28. Since arriving at Oregon High School, Mr. Caposey and the school have received many honors, including winning the Illinois Principal's Association/Horace Mann Partners in Education Award and being named one of the nation's top high schools by U.S. News and World Report. Mr. Caposey has received the Award of Merit from the Those Who Excel program, sponsored by the Illinois State Board of Education. He has also been honored as an exemplar candidate for the ASCD Outstanding Young Educator Award.

Currently, Mr. Caposey is pursuing his doctoral degree at Western Illinois University and continuing to write and guest blog for many websites such as ASCD, Edutopia, and Test Soup. He has also presented at many local, state, and national conferences and has served in different consultative capacities for schools and other organizations. In addition, Mr. Caposey is an adjunct professor for the educational leadership department at Aurora University.

Mr. Caposey still serves as the Oregon High School principal. He is married with two children and resides in the Northwestern part of Illinois. He can be reached at principalcaposey@hotmail.com or @principalpc on Twitter.

CONTENTS

INTRODUCTION

*Change comes when teachers are personally committed to the work of becoming better and better at teaching. And it comes most enduringly when that commitment exists in an open and thoughtful context that **supports** the work.*

—*Carolyn Bunting*

At a national conference in the fall of 2011, I had a conversation with a fellow educator that impacted me significantly. Most attendees at the conference were faculty from colleges and universities, which alone was enough to stretch a K–12 educator's comfort zone. My presentation, scheduled for 8 a.m. on Saturday morning (the least favorable of presentation slots), discussed, among other things, the common perception that American public schools are failing. During the conclusion of my presentation, a particularly interactive attendee offered a critique. The gentleman asked the question: "Who says the American public education system is failing?" The more appropriate question in my mind is—who doesn't?

The current, and past, education reform movements in America are based on the concept that schools are failing and through media rhetoric often propagate the fear that America is losing its place among the global educational elite. My belief is that policy changes and reform movements intended to create educational change are failing at a more alarming rate than any American public school. They are failing because policy change and large-scale reform have not been able create lasting, meaningful change to support school improvement. School leaders are needed to facilitate this change. Now, more than at any time in the past, teachers need and deserve the support and guidance of strong leaders. The idea that one-size-fits-all accountability and transparency measures will create meaningful change in the way schools educate students is ludicrous.

Education is changing at an exponential rate today compared to any other time in history, but contrary to the belief of educational pundits, American education has not gotten worse. However, education in other parts of the world is getting better—faster (Stewart, 2012). The explosion of technology, the erosion of the 1950s standard for family living, the dramatically different postsecondary school options for employment, and the globalization of the economy have not only fundamentally changed the way we must educate students, but also expanded the role schools must play in our society to prepare students for life in the global marketplace.

Schools need to improve. Schools need to change. We know this; however, we also know that the current means of school improvement, which are influenced more by politics, media, and the big business of educational professional development than by common sense, have yielded minimal results at best.

> Meaningful change in education occurs at a local level. Meaningful change in schools happens because of you. It happens as a result of dedicated and passionate people who understand how to lead change and have the courage to do so.

Despite the many volumes of research done on all things educational—from instructional strategies to behavior to assessment to demographics to curriculum—there is no single model that works at every school every time. If there was, every school in the country would be using it! School improvement is simply more complex than people, especially outside the world of education, want to admit. For schools to meet the unprecedented challenge of helping all students learn at high levels, educators must establish very different school cultures. Structural changes—changes in policy, programs, and procedures—will only take a school so far (DuFour, 2006, p. 1).

A working session with a group of administrators and teachers from my region commenced with the question, "How many of your schools are 'doing' professional learning communities?" Almost every hand shot up. The follow-up question asked how many people were observing meaningful change in their schools as a result of this process. Not one hand went up in a sizable group of people. This situation indicates precisely why American schools are struggling to improve.

The problem is not the improvement model. The problem is not the research. The problem is not that people in education do not know the textbook answer to fix the problem. The problem is not that educators are lazy. The problem is that no single program, initiative, or improvement model can be properly implemented without a culture of support in a school or district firmly in place.

As the saying goes, "a person's character is defined by who that person is when nobody is watching." Similarly, school culture is what defines your school when nobody is watching. School culture is how your school operates on a daily basis—from the principal's office to the classroom to the lunchroom to the maintenance den. Many school leaders, policy-makers, and communities eager for change have neglected to realize that instituting any new program, intervention, or policy before first establishing a culture of support is the equivalent to planting tomato seeds in the desert. Without the appropriate environment, implementing a new program or initiative is simply a waste of teacher and administrator energy and time. The good news, however, remains that environments are malleable and change is possible. As a result, schools can improve, but we must begin to lead that change today! We must be the change we want to see in our schools!

1

Fostering a Culture of Support

Vision, Mission, and Goals

Vision can be both directly impacted by and conceived through the context of the times. Vision divorced from context can produce very erratic and unpredictable results. . . . Leaders . . . can and do shape the parameters for success through a vision for a future. And, just as important, they possess the ability to oversee that vision's implementation.

—*Tony Mayo*

Craig Trissler is a high school principal in Smithville, Missouri—an area too large to be considered rural, but certainly not urban, or even suburban. Recently, the economic struggles facing the country took their toll on Smithville High School and inevitably Mr. Trissler was forced to make reductions in staff. However, he felt fortunate that despite the impending staff cuts, he would not be forced to cut any programs or remove any class options for students. Unfortunately, once the scheduling process for the upcoming year commenced, it became clear that nine talented 12th-grade students would be left with holes in their schedules as a result of the very tight scheduling caused by the staffing cuts.

Mr. Trissler had some options: he could lobby the superintendent and Board of Education for an additional instructional aide and begin offering study halls at Smithville HS; he could allow those students to become teacher's assistants; or he could get creative and attempt to enrich these students' experiences. He knew that seeking enrichment activities for his students was the most student-centered option, but he was struggling to get the process started. Around the same time, he received a request from some local businessmen and community activists with political clout for the high school to focus some attention on the history of the community. Mr. Trissler had the resources (students) to accommodate this desire. That request created the perfect enrichment opportunity for the nine students. Mr. Trissler envisioned a project that would "stretch" the students, so he viewed this opportunity as a win-win situation.

Mr. Trissler approached the handful of students with this potential project and they were excited to participate. The students would be enrolled in an independent study class with Mr. Trissler himself serving as the instructor. This left Mr. Trissler with another unprecedented decision to make. He could define an end product to guide the class or he could extend his students' learning opportunity further by providing them with an open-ended assignment, therefore forcing them to be leaders in addition to being students. Given the caliber of the students and the time frame for completion, he was confident that the students would eventually be successful with only a skeleton of expectations to work from.

At the first meeting, Mr. Trissler provided the nine students with a syllabus outlining the topic and some blanket expectations. The expectations were simple: students were to proactively communicate with the principal every two weeks and some product was to be ready for public consumption within eight months. Furthermore, the students would receive a collective grade for the entire group dependent upon the quality of the product. As a result, the quality of the product would be dependent upon the collaborative effort of all the students.

The group decided to construct a website for the effort and embed interviews that took place with many influential people throughout the community. The biweekly communications, however, revealed results counter to what Mr. Trissler originally expected and a case study of leadership emerged. Students who typically had no problem getting along with everybody suddenly could not get along with each other. Some of the students celebrated the autonomy given to them by doing absolutely nothing, leaving the others with no idea how to motivate their peers. After some time, the students doing the heavy lifting became extremely agitated, but refused to confront their colleagues. Eventually, the students' frustration and angst rose enough that they sought out Mr. Trissler to address the issue. Mr. Trissler met with each student individually and once as a team in order to gain a firm understanding of what was transpiring. He concluded that the group had not been provided with enough direction and, as a result,

- The group of students felt helpless and did not know how to begin the process.
- Roles within the group were not defined, and people were reluctant to assume leadership.
- Without defined leadership, accountability for all waned.
- Without a clear end product to work toward, many aspects of the project were meandering, done with little enthusiasm, and unlikely to fit into the final product.
- Relationships and capacity had actually diminished from the onset of the project.

Although Mr. Trissler's situation involved students, the same complications occur when a school leader fails to establish an overall goal and performance expectations for adults in the school. *This breakdown of a team is precisely why adhering to the principles of a school's mission statement and collaboratively establishing a vision is essential for school success.* Mission and vision statements provide purpose and goals for a school—exactly what was missing from the project constructed by Mr. Trissler.

Great principals do not allow the complications that arose in the process described above to impact their school and their staff. Principals who continually focus on activities that support mission-based decision-making and embrace a collective vision serve to constantly energize and reinvigorate their schools. Schools that are not currently driven by a mission and vision have an outstanding opportunity to create substantial momentum moving toward a culture of support by engaging in renewal activities. When done appropriately, these renewal activities may serve a purpose for a school similar in nature to a baptism. The benefits are twofold; not only does the process give renewed vigor and life to the school, but it also resolves many of the leadership grievances that occurred in the past by allowing the staff to collaboratively decide upon the intended direction of the organization. This process by itself does not change a culture or lead to school improvement, however. Isolated from objective goals and benchmarks, establishing a vision is simply the process of identifying two spots on a map. Any five-year-old can do that. Being able to establish the most efficient and effective way to get from Point A to Point B is an entirely different, and more difficult, proposition, and that is the responsibility of the principal.

Rule 1

As baseball great Yogi Berra once said, if you don't know where you are going, you are probably not going to get there. School leaders who are able to create meaningful and sustained change have not only an end in mind, but also the foresight to align their efforts and create action plans to achieve their goals. SUPPORT THE VISION, MISSION, AND GOALS.

The Professionals

The quality of an education system cannot exceed the quality of its teachers and the only way to improve student outcomes is to improve instruction.

—McKinsey & Company

My first administrative job was in a very unique school. With an enrollment of about 2,000 students, the school had a separate ninth-grade campus, drew from the worst socioeconomic area of an urban area, and also housed the performing arts and gifted programs for a district of over 50 schools. Upon my arrival at the school, my primary responsibility was discipline, but I still had a desire to work in classrooms and help teachers improve instruction. Not surprisingly, my exuberant desire to be in the classroom (which did not match the culture of the building) was not universally well received. A few months into my first year, I had a conversation with a very competent veteran teacher, whom I liked very much, regarding some of her instructional practices I had observed earlier in the day. As the conversation began to wane, she shook her head and stated that she believed I would move on to bigger and better opportunities shortly, but she had begun her career at that school and would end it there as well. Then she looked at me and said, "Before you try and make any big changes around here, remember that you may be visiting this building, but we [the teachers] live here." At first I was taken aback, even angered, by this statement, but the more experiences I gain, the more I understand the paradigm from which that teacher was operating. She had every right to fear change implemented by a single person because change brought on by one person, or solely by administration, is destined for failure. Successful leaders can accomplish sustainable change only by serving those involved, not creating something in spite of them.

Even the most effective school should be in a constant state of adaptation and change; otherwise both teachers and administrators soon find that they are performing beneath the high standard that they created for themselves. School change is a difficult, complex process. Change is hard for people because it involves loss, whether it is the loss of a privilege, a level of comfort, or something more tangible. People are not frustrated by new ideas being brought to the table; they are simply hesitant to abandon the old concepts, ideas, or programs they have grown comfortable in using or implementing. The principal's support for staff members already engrained in their current culture through the change process is the difference between a cultural shift that will have a lasting impact and yet another failed education program or initiative.

It is only with tremendous leadership that schools can improve in a systematic and sustainable manner. Leadership within a school or district must refer not only to administration, but also to faculty and staff. If the change process is entirely dependent upon administration, the success will be, at best, short-lived. Leadership must provide faculty and staff the opportunities they deserve to function as an essential component of successful school improvement. The process of supporting individuals and striving to align personal goals to organizational goals is complex, but it is exactly what is needed to provide for the changed culture that will allow for true school improvement.

Rule 2

Building and district-level leadership alone cannot create meaningful and sustained change. The only way for achievement to improve is for instruction to improve. SUPPORT THE PROFESSIONALS.

The Students

Never underestimate the power of students. For decades, some of the most creative and breakthrough ideas have come not from CEOs and power brokers but from students who didn't let anything hold them back. And what's also interesting is that they always have.

—Joe Wilson

The purpose of education is fairly simple at its core. Yet when people think about the purpose of education, they often become distracted by the buzzwords of policy-makers and media members. The purpose of education is *not* to close the achievement gap, leave no child behind, race to the top, or create students who are college and career ready. The purpose of education is to maximize the capacity of every student who walks through our school doors. Fostering this belief and the culture of support to make this possible is the true essence of leading change in today's schools. This paradigm shift toward being learner-centered is what separates average teachers from great teachers and average schools from great schools. A commitment to pushing all our kids as far as they can individually go is what defines effective education.

American education is starting to lose what has made it truly unique over the past 60 years and what has helped to place America at the front of the global economic and power races. Students deserve to be supported by forward-thinking, 21st-century schools and leaders. Winning the battle of standardized test scores is not nearly as important as remaining the highest volume producer of the most innovative, creative, and socially aware students.

American schools have never served a more at-risk population or a population coming from a lower socioeconomic status. Educators know that the chances of students being exposed to cultural experiences ranging from the zoo to the art institute to the museum to simple suburban life are at an all-time low. Yet as money becomes tight, far too often (as a result of poor fiscal management and protection of pet programs) the first programs to be cut are field trips and the arts.

In schools that have been managed well enough to sustain these key programs, they are still the areas that students are commonly pulled from to receive instruction as part of a Response to Intervention (RtI) program. These decisions are often made without thorough analysis of the quality of the instruction being provided in the room or of the instructor providing intervention. A program with data-based evidence of success or an acclaimed curriculum implemented by a poor teacher will produce poor results. The desire to be on board with the latest initiative discussed in a professional journal or focused on at conferences often causes school leaders to move forward without recognizing why the program is necessary in the first place. *Far too often, schools treat the symptoms of dysfunction as opposed to the causes.*

These rushed and pressured decisions are being made by well-intentioned leaders throughout the country every day. The intent of subsequent chapters is to guide building leaders to break down how best to support students in the current educational environment. Supporting students and being truly learner-centered calls for a change in focus. Switching the focus from maximizing student performance on a subset of standardized tests to truly maximizing student capacity is a trait that bonds highly successful schools and highly successful school leaders. That concept, which promotes creativity and ingenuity, is what has made America great and what will continue to make America great. That is how great leaders seek to prepare students for the challenges of the 21st century.

Rule 3

Maximizing test scores is not equivalent to maximizing student capacity. Principals need to remain focused on what the true priority should be. SUPPORT THE STUDENTS.

The Community

The foundation of every state is the education of its youth.
—*Diogenes Laertius*

Schools must believe it is their job to serve the community, not the community's job to serve them. School improvement cannot be quantified in a manner that is universally statistically constant and easily digestible by those people who do not understand the processes of education—that is, the media and the politicians. What makes a school in the Bronx great would not make a school in Appalachia great and would certainly not make a school in the wealthiest suburbs of Chicago great. It is, however, possible for every school in this country to truly improve and better serve its community. To do so, the principal and staff of each school must begin to foster a culture of support.

My work in inner-city schools, urban schools, and rural schools has made abundantly clear to me the role and responsibility that the school should play in supporting the community. Many educators speak of how their schools could improve if they received support from the outside when their paradigm should be exactly the opposite. If schools wait to improve practice until full community support exists, schools will be sitting stagnant for an awfully long time. School and community relationships need to change now and it is the principal's responsibility to initiate such change.

Schools also have the potential to bring great pride to any area. This is not an easy proposition. While most communities support their local schools, the focus on standardized test scores and reporting of such have left many communities and schools feeling "average." School leaders throughout the country are acutely aware of the power of those presuppositions. Changing these perceptions is paramount for school leaders. Schools, after all, are a reflection of the community and vice versa. Changing that perception as quickly as possible is vitally important. Parents, students, and other community members understand a school's true strengths and weaknesses. It is vital for the principal to tap into that knowledge with confidence because every community wants a great school, just as all parents want what is best for their children. The role of the school leader is to support the parents in that end.

Schools also can serve a community simply through manpower. Maintaining a healthy and thriving community, especially in lower socioeconomic areas, simply requires more resources than are available. Schools, through structured opportunities and incentive programs, can form dynamic partnerships with other government agencies that can lead to near-immediate change in communities and in school images. Schools need to be the change they want to see in their communities.

Rule 4

The school must be the change it wants to see in the community. This can be achieved with pro-active planning and commitment. SUPPORT THE COMMUNITY

2

The Vision, Mission, and Goals

Starting from the Ground Up

You've got to be very careful if you don't know where you're going because you're probably not going to get there.

— Yogi Berra

By consciously starting with the end in mind, an effective principal can move to the forefront the things that should truly be important to a school and community—enacting the vision and mission of the school or district. Mission statements attempt to articulate the purpose of why schools exist and are foundational to the future success of societies. They often discuss creating lifelong learners, responsible citizenry, and preparing students for life in a global community. Creating an environment dedicated to supporting the enactment of these lofty ideals builds a healthy culture that allows principals to appropriately frame the many tasks, trials, and tribulations they face through a lens that provides clarity and meaning.

Serving as a building leader is without a doubt an incredibly difficult job. Contrary to what many outsiders (and some principals) may believe, principals truly have little control over what takes place in a school. Principals may have tremendous influence, but they have little control. Realizing this can create a great deal of discomfort for most leaders, since by nature most principals (especially those with alpha personalities) desire to be in control. The only thing all principals can truly control is their own behavior, and by doing so while committing to a servant-leadership model focused on supporting the mission and vision, as mentioned above, as well as the professionals in the building, students, and the community (as discussed in later chapters), principals can constantly expand their influence and begin building a culture of support.

No school is sitting stagnant. Every school is trying to improve. The unfortunate truth is that while everybody desires improvement, few schools are experiencing the desired results. The words of the secretary of education, Arne Duncan, are quite strong on the subject. Referring to the disappointing results of the 2009 Programme for International Student Assessment (PISA), in which the United States finished in the mid-20s, he said, "We have to see this as a wake-up call. I know skeptics will want to argue with the results, but we consider them to be accurate and reliable, and we have to see them as a challenge to get better. . . . The United States came in 23rd or 24th in most subjects. We can quibble, or we can face the brutal truth that we're being out-educated" (Dillon, 2010). School leaders are listening to the words of Mr. Duncan. Engaged principals throughout the nation are attempting to lead change in their buildings with the best, most well-researched programs available. Schools, however, continue to struggle.

The question why must be asked.

School Culture Defined

I believe that the answer to the question is simple. No improvement plan, initiative, or program is strong enough to overcome an unhealthy school culture. Culture is to a school what character is to an individual. It is the set of qualities that makes a school distinct from others. Culture is defined within a school by its values, priorities, and ethos. Most importantly, school cultures are malleable, and through the work of outstanding school leaders, cultures can and do change.

Before attempting to make any changes in a school, a school leader must first accurately assess the current situation, otherwise known as performing a self-audit. The purpose of this audit is to analyze a school's culture: the current beliefs and values held by the school personnel and how they impact behavior. Self-assessment may seem like a simple concept, but given the humanistic nature of schools, it can prove extremely difficult.

When completing a self-audit, principals must ask difficult questions and collaboratively discuss the state of the school with their faculty and staff. This process can be even more difficult if those involved contributed to the current state of the school. The questions below serve as a functional audit for any school at any time. Questions can be added or subtracted to fit the specific needs of a given school in order to procure the information that will effect change:

- ♦ Does a guiding set of principles or values influence all decisions made in the building?
- ♦ If so, do all stakeholders know exactly what the guiding principles are?
- ♦ Does our school have a mission *and* vision statement?
- ♦ Are the guiding principles articulated through the mission statement and will they allow for our school to enact its vision?
- ♦ Do the vast majority of staff members filter daily decision-making (for example, in classroom activities, lesson planning, and discipline) through that lens (mission and vision)?
- ♦ Do all our current school improvement goals align with both the vision and mission?
- ♦ Does the intended purpose of our vision and mission statements define our school's culture?

Working through this process can produce humbling news. What the news is does not matter (initially); what you, as the leader, do with the information is what is important. Very few schools are able to answer yes to every question. As these questions are asked, the information provided by your faculty and staff will serve to answer the very first question that needs to be answered to improve your school and its culture—where do you currently stand? While simply asking the questions is not enough to improve a school, it does serve to establish a sense of purpose or urgency. Your role as principal is to lead this investigatory process to determine the current state of the school. This process of conducting a self-audit allows leaders to establish a sense of greater purpose and, if necessary, confront the brutal facts in order to move their buildings forward.

Aligning Under a Mission Statement

Just about every school district has a mission statement. Whether that mission statement is meaningful remains the question. Most school mission statements are similar in content and purpose and convey a very altruistic message that discusses much more than academic achievement alone. Previously in this chapter the culture of a school was likened to the character of a person and described as being defined by values, priorities, and ethos. Mission statements intend to articulate just those things: values, priorities, and ethos.

Regardless of the quality of the mission statement, it only becomes meaningful when the behaviors and decision-making within a school serve to enact the purpose of the words on the piece of paper, letterhead, or banner. Simply adding the words of a mission statement below the signature line of an e-mail will not do that. Hanging a framed version of the Ten Commandments does not make the local watering hole a holy place—hanging a framed mission statement on the wall of a school without committing to working toward its true meaning is equally ineffective at creating change.

This is where a great leadership challenge presents itself. Most schools and school leaders have very little influence over the mission statement they operate under. Creating a mission statement is generally reserved as a right of the board of education. As principal, you serve as an agent of the board of education, and thus your charge is to work toward enacting the mission. The role of the principal in this case is not to work collaboratively to create a mission statement, but to act as an agent of alignment. This is one time when the flowery, vague language often associated with mission statements is beneficial. The principal must work with the staff to unwrap the language of the statement and to identify the purpose, values, and behaviors that can be promoted to bring its altruistic goals to life.

For a mission statement to serve its purpose, for it to have a strong, positive impact on the culture of the school, building leaders must support it as a driving influence upon decision-making practices. A mission statement becomes important the moment it becomes a point of emphasis for a building leader. When a leader becomes effective at supporting a healthy, sustainable culture, the mission statement becomes the lens through which decisions are made. This is something you have absolute control over!

Principals can facilitate this alignment in one of two ways:

Option One:

1. At a faculty meeting or professional development activity, provide a copy of the mission statement at the top of a handout with plenty of white space below.

2. Ask the group of teachers to decode the mission statement on their own, identify what principles and values are embodied within that group of words, and write them in the available white space.

3. After some time, have the group share their responses and discuss whether they agree or disagree.

4. Establish a consensus list.

5. Pose this question: Is there anything on this list we do not believe in?
   a. If the answer is yes, discuss whether that item is interpretation or philosophy. If interpretation, reexamine the issue. If philosophy, ask whether it is good for kids and then reexamine.
   b. If the answer is no, move on.

6. Pose this question: Is there anything we want to achieve that we are precluded from as a result of abiding by these principles?

a. If the answer is yes, thoroughly scrutinize the idea. If the idea does not match the building mission, it may be a great idea, just not great for you.

b. If the answer is no, the process is complete.

Option Two:

1. Begin a meeting by asking the faculty to outline the principles and values of the organization (this can be done in any way that works best with your faculty and staff).

2. Create a consensus list.

3. Unveil the mission statement prominently.

4. Ask if there is anything that the staff values that is not encompassed by the mission statement.

5. Pose this question: Is there anything we want to achieve that we are precluded from as a result of abiding by these principles?

The success of an organization is often determined by the alignment of individual goals with those of the organization. In day-to-day written and face-to-face interactions, the principal should aim to create a sense of commitment and value in working toward the mission statement as an overarching, altruistic end in mind. This commitment to an agreed-upon end serves to dramatically extend the influence of the principal while simultaneously improving the school culture.

As an example, read this scenario and imagine the difference in effectiveness and power between the two statements that follow:

> Sam Smith comes to the office at Jayhawk Elementary in tears because his math teacher, Mr. Tremble, refuses to let him make up a test that brought his grade from a B to a C. Sam tried to explain to Mr. Tremble that he failed the assessment because his parents were up all night in a shouting match and he could not get to sleep. Subsequent intervention work with Sam confirmed this to be true. When Mr. Tremble was asked about the situation, he replied, "I don't get do-overs. Why should the kids?"

Principal's Response 1: "Mr. Tremble, allowing retakes is a best practice and in this case just makes sense. I encourage you to consider that."

Principal's Response 2: "We, as a faculty at our opening day meeting, decided that our driving purpose was to enact our mission statement and abide by our guiding principles. One of those principles is being learner-centered. Since your behavior in this case does not promote the mission statement, is not learner-centered, and does not reflect best practices, I cannot support your decision."

Both responses essentially state the same thing; however, since the second response discusses collaborative alignment under an agreed-upon goal, the power of the statement, as well as the influence of the principal, is exponentially greater compared to the first response.

Creating or Confirming a Vision Statement

While the mission statement is occasionally an afterthought in some schools, at least it exists. The same cannot be said for schools when it comes to vision statements. The power of vision statements is evident, however. As a building leader, you need to inform and educate your staff regarding the potential impact of a vision statement. Stephen Covey made popular the phrase "Begin with the end in mind" years ago as a key to personal success; the same sentiment holds true for any school or organization. As a principal, you must set the course for your building.

Vision statements are timely, meaning they must fit the given situation of your building. The process as outlined throughout this chapter—performing a self-audit, aligning under a mission statement, and creating or confirming a vision statement—should occur in that prescribed order. Establishing a vision is an empowering activity to complete as a team—and does not create the stress of completing a self-audit. A vision statement, however, can be a difficult concept to introduce and explain adequately as a result of its similarity to a mission statement. It is prudent for a leader to understand this complexity and tread slowly through this process. While complex, the process is rewarding. When the building principal calls upon a faculty and staff to envision what they truly want their school to be, the discussion that begins creates optimism and passion moving forward. A sample handout that could be used with any faculty and staff to support the process is provided below:

"Vision-ing"

A mission statement can be defined as a sentence or short paragraph written to reflect the school's core purpose, identity, values, and principal aims. For example: *"Educate students to be lifelong learners who are productive, responsible citizens."*

A vision statement can be defined as a sentence or short paragraph providing a broad, aspirational image of the future. For example: *"To become the premier small school in the state."*

Examples of vision statements from prominent organizations:

ANHEUSER-BUSCH: Be the world's beer company. Through all of our products, services and relationships, we will add to life's enjoyment.

BOEING, 1950: Become the dominant player in commercial aircraft and bring the world into the jet age.

FORD, EARLY 1900s: Democratize the automobile.

FORD, CURRENTLY: To become the world's leading consumer company for automotive products and services.

NIKE, 1960s: Crush Adidas.

NIKE, CURRENTLY: To be the number one athletic company in the world.

STANFORD UNIVERSITY, 1940s: Become the Harvard of the West.

VOLKSWAGEN: By 2018 the Volkswagen Group is to be the world's most successful and fascinating automobile manufacturer— and the leading light when it comes to sustainability.

Examples of vision statements from schools:

UNIVERSITY HIGH SCHOOL (IRVINE, CALIFORNIA): University High School will provide students with the means to acquire knowledge and develop habits of mind to prepare them for the world they will inherit. (University High School, n.d.)

KENNEDY MIDDLE SCHOOL (PHARR, TEXAS): Kennedy Middle School is committed to ensuring that all students are prepared for high school and college by reaching their highest potential in meeting their academic, social, and emotional needs. (Kennedy Middle School, n.d.)

MARTIN LUTHER KING HIGH SCHOOL (RIVERSIDE, CALIFORNIA): Martin Luther King High School's vision is to excel by developing an educational environment which will transform lives and communities. We aim for each student to develop a willingness to explore ideas and become responsible citizens in today's global society. (Martin Luther King High School, n.d.)

BAKER ELEMENTARY SCHOOL (ALTOONA, PENNSYLVANIA): Baker Elementary School will strive for quality education through innovative and creative methods of service, respect for all people and collaboration through shared participation and mutual responsibility. (Altoona Area School District, n.d.)

The role of a principal in introducing the concept of vision statements is similar to that of a teacher. The first goal is for the faculty and staff to have a firm understanding of what a great vision statement looks like:

- ♦ Vision statements are succinct.
- ♦ Vision statements are timely—meaning relevant to the given state of the organization.
- ♦ Vision statements are extremely personal to the organization.

The principal then must work to impact the mind-set of the faculty and staff. While principals spend a great deal of time and energy thinking about and planning the future for their schools, this is not something most teachers spent mental energy on. For the vision-ing process to truly be collaborative, the principal must facilitate staff members' thinking in such a way. Multiple prompts can be given to staff members to encourage this process. A handful are listed below, but many more exist that may be equally, if not more, effective depending on the individual staff you are working with. Remember, as with all things in education, one size does not fit all: what works well for a high school staff may not work well for the elementary staff in a building located directly across the street.

- Have small groups of teachers write an article for the paper describing the state of the school five years from now if everything goes according to plan. Detail what has been accomplished and what they would want the public to know.
- Create a scroll and ask staff members as a whole group to fill in the past events that have led to the current situation. Then encourage those staff members who are willing to fill in the future.
- A couple of weeks before the meeting, ask faculty to provide one-paragraph answers to the question "Why did you decide to teach?" As the meeting commences, play a simple, slow-moving slide show with all the answers displayed anonymously. Discuss the lofty ideals displayed and ask "If we all worked to that level, what would the future of our school look like?"
- Start with simple icebreaker questions: "If you were a house, what kind of house would you be? Why? If you were a car, what kind of car would you be? Why?" This can extend for however long you like; then state, "We are a school—what kind of school would you like to be?"

These conversations may evolve and devolve into many different things depending on the current state of your building. It is important to remember that the vision is a collaboratively agreed-upon end, so all desired outcomes must be discussed and addressed directly by the teachers as a group. Ideally, through this stage the building leader will serve as a facilitator, but occasionally your role may adapt to that of mediator or even salesperson. The process should be collaborative in nature, but as the building leader you also have a vested interest in the direction of the conversation. The desired outcome of the initial stages of developing a vision is to simply agree upon a set of principles that the staff want incorporated into a vision statement.

Once principles are decided upon—get out of the way. Provide guidelines, timelines, and norms and let the staff own the process (see Figure 2.1). Be patient!

"The Oregon High School vision is to be the premier small school in the state of Illinois." To get to that statement took a group of highly intelligent and extremely effective educators two and a half *months*! A similar amount of time will be well spent in your

Figure 2.1   Re: Vision Writing Committee

Good afternoon, Faculty and Staff:

I would first like to thank each of you for attending the voluntary meeting that took place this afternoon to discuss the development of a vision statement for Stanford Elementary School. The meeting was very productive and I feel that we were able to leave the meeting with a collaborative understanding of what a vision statement is and why it is vital to our organization to develop one. After working in small groups for some time, we were able to leave the meeting with a consensus set of principles that the committee will attempt to interweave into a vision statement for our school. The work of the committee will keep in mind the following:

Guidelines:
1. One representative from each grade level will be on the committee.
2. Please inform me who will be representing your grade level by the end of next week.
3. The committee will select a chair who will lead communication, set meeting dates, and communicate with administration.
4. The principles _____, _____, _____, and _____, as decided at the meeting today, will be the focus of the vision writing process. The vision statement should be succinct, timely (meaning relevant to the given state of the school), and extremely personal to the school.

Timelines:
1. The committee will meet twice per month starting in September. Times and dates will be set at the convenience of members. Administrators will not attend unless requested by the group.
2. The expectation is that a draft statement will be ready for review by parents, students, and staff by November.
3. Once feedback is received, revisions (if necessary) will be made.
4. The revised statement will be sent back to the original groups for additional revision.
5. Once the statement is approved by those groups, it will be introduced to the staff as a whole group.
6. The goal is to complete writing the vision statement by the end of this semester.

Norms:
1. This is a staff-driven, collaborative process.
2. The committee chair will function not as an authority, but as an organizer and liaison.
3. The overarching purpose should be stated at each meeting and all activities should lead to that end.

Thank you in advance for your hard work.

Kim LeFrank
Stanford Elementary Principal

school. Having the staff create a vision statement that completely encompasses what your school wants for itself provides clarity and an opportunity for the building leader to extend influence. Since the inception of Oregon High's vision statement, many conversations start with a comparison of current behaviors and decision-making with those of a premier or elite school. This process has allowed many conversations that once barely lasted 60 seconds to have a substantially more influential outcome. Enforcing norms is no longer an issue of doing what the administration says; it becomes acting in accordance with what the staff desires.

School Improvement Plans

As anybody who has ever worked out or been on a diet knows, simply stating that you want to get ripped, get fit, get healthy, slim down, or bulk up does little to improve your chances of achieving the goal. In order to move forward, you must set goals and create concrete plans on how to achieve each goal. Most schools already have a system for completing this process in place, the school improvement process that results in the creation of a school improvement plan (SIP). A SIP should serve as the equivalent of a comprehensive business plan—identifying goals, deciding how and when they will be measured to determine success, and outlining the steps towards each benchmark. The SIP provides the tangible steps to achieve the lofty ideals of the vision and mission. Goals within an improvement plan need to be directly aligned to the vision and mission of the organization and should thus drive all organizational activity. The ridiculousness of having the goal of getting lean and fit and then eating fast food as part of the action plan does not seem so otherworldly when examining some improvement plans and their alignment to the school's vision and mission.

School improvement plans are the grounded, practical applications set in place to enact the mission and vision of a building. When aligned properly (as this section will describe), a school improvement plan turns the abstract to the concrete and allows for a written plan to impact the culture of a school. The appropriate process is represented in Figure 2.2 (page 28).

Identifying Goals

In the world of education and school improvement, all goals are not created equal. A goal that is not measurable becomes little more than a wish or a hope. A goal that is timely, measurable, and attainable, however, can serve to drive school improvement (see Figure 2.3, page 29).

Figure 2.2 School Improvement Plan Process

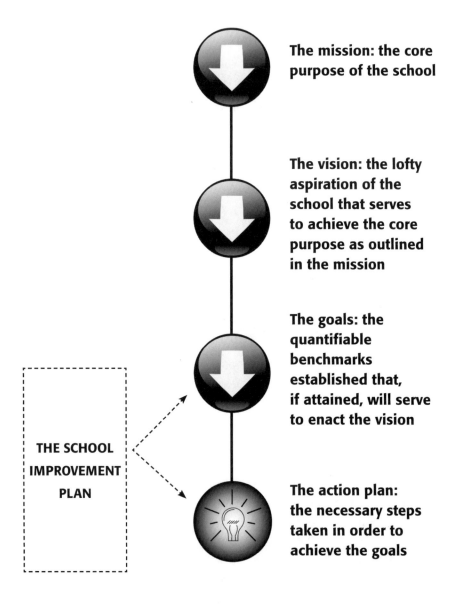

The mission: the core purpose of the school

The vision: the lofty aspiration of the school that serves to achieve the core purpose as outlined in the mission

The goals: the quantifiable benchmarks established that, if attained, will serve to enact the vision

THE SCHOOL IMPROVEMENT PLAN

The action plan: the necessary steps taken in order to achieve the goals

Figure 2.3 Goal Comparison

General Goal	Goal That Can Drive School Improvement
Adopt Common Core State Standards	Improve the current core curricula as measured by an 85% alignment to the Common Core State Standards in all core area classes by spring of 2013
Better align student behavior to mission	To better prepare students for responsible citizenry by reducing the number of discipline referrals by 10% and increasing the number of community service hours by 15% each year until 2015
Increase academic achievement	Increase the percentage of students reaching growth targets on national assessment by 5% each year until 2016
Promote better instructional pedagogy	Documentation from informal and formal observations will note an increase in proficient or distinguished use of questioning and assessment strategies by 10% compared to an average of the past two school years

In addition to being written in a format that can drive school improvement, there must be a direct link between the achievement of the stated goals and the enactment of the stated vision and mission of the school. This may cause a number of quality initiatives, programs, and goals to be expelled from a school's improvement plan. Some goals, programs, and initiatives are great, just not great for your particular school at this particular time. Highly effective schools and school leaders have the ability and courage to say no to *en vogue* or trendy school initiatives. Following the simple flowchart in Figure 2.4 (page 30) will support the school improvement process.

Falling in love with ideas or concepts is an easy trap for leaders to fall into. Great leaders do not simply accept the status quo, but rather constantly seek improvements. This has led to an overabundance of programs and initiatives that are research-based and have

Figure 2.4 Goal Flowchart

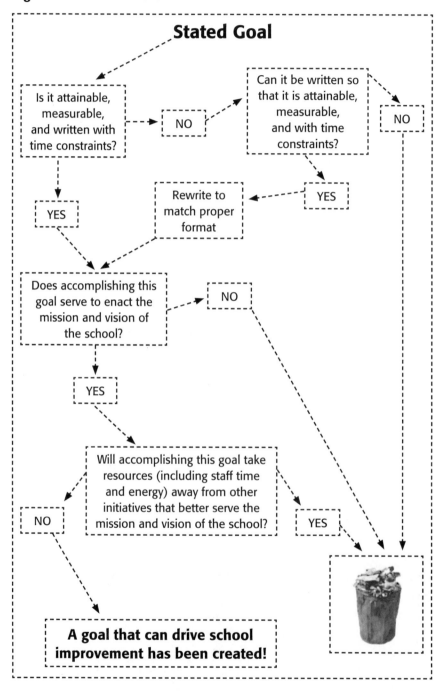

Stated Goal

Is it attainable, measurable, and written with time constraints?

NO

Can it be written so that it is attainable, measurable, and with time constraints?

NO

YES

YES

Rewrite to match proper format

Does accomplishing this goal serve to enact the mission and vision of the school?

NO

YES

Will accomplishing this goal take resources (including staff time and energy) away from other initiatives that better serve the mission and vision of the school?

NO

YES

A goal that can drive school improvement has been created!

been successful in some schools but have not proven beneficial for others. Therefore, the fit—not the attractiveness of the program itself—should be the most important factor when determining whether to add new programs. Three things should be considered when examining fit: alignment, resources, and sustainability (see Figure 2.5).

Figure 2.5 Example Analysis

Program: Introducing Mandarin as a Foreign Language	
Alignment	Principals must vet each new initiative through the lens of the mission and vision of their school. Mandarin Chinese is viewed by many as the future language of international business. Therefore, schools with mission statements that discuss supporting their students in order to be competitive in a global society may want to introduce Mandarin as a language option for students. Schools whose current vision may be solely on advancing math and reading proficiency at the current time would not see adding Mandarin as a prudent move in terms of alignment to mission and vision.
Resources	Initiatives and programs almost always have a cost—either in terms of money, resources, or both. The cost of a program should be analyzed after the principal has determined that it aligns with the vision and mission statements of the school. Mandarin is a good fit for schools that have the financial means to add a program without eliminating another. It is also a good fit for schools that could replace a current program that that is not significantly benefiting students as indicated by data or an audit of alignment with the mission and vision or one that has not garnered student interest. Mandarin does not fit well in a school that already has limited funding and thus cannot add a program without eliminating an already successful one.
Sustainability	Educators who are constantly exposed to "flavor of the month" programs find it hard to approach each

Sustainability (*continued*)	new initiative with the same zeal after repeated instances of program changes. As a building leader, it is important to consider whether or not a program is sustainable before exposing your staff to the change.
	Schools that have a solid funding source and a commitment to teaching Mandarin, despite expected low enrollment at the commencement of the program, should continue to progress through the process.
	Schools that have a non-sustainable funding source (grant money) or anticipate financial hardship that could impact whether or not the program is kept should not proceed. Enrollment must also be considered: What is the minimum number of students taking this course required to make it a worthwhile initiative?

Highly effective principals scrutinize each decision and have the courage to state, "While this may be a great program/idea/initiative; it is not great for our current situation and I will not divert our resources of time, money, and energy away from our other goals at this time." Such a statement clearly indicates that the building leaders desire to truly serve students and teachers in a school by serving the mission and vision of the school.

Steps You Can Take to Support the Vision, Mission, and Goals

Effective school leaders do two things exceptionally well: maximize the capacity of each of their employees (as will be discussed at length in Chapter 3) and align the personal goals of employees to the goals of the organization. The most deeply motivated people—not to mention those who are most productive and satisfied—hitch their desires to a cause larger than themselves (Pink, 2009). To align personal goals with school goals, the principal must make a steadfast effort to support staff understanding of what the school goals are. Ensuring staff understanding of the school improvement goals can be achieved in a three-step process:

1. Weekly e-mails updating data and action plans for different goals should be sent to staff. Addressing each goal and action plan every week is too cumbersome and time-consuming in most instances, but each week the entire faculty and staff should be updated as to the progress toward a segment of the plan. The primary focus of this correspondence sent from the principal is to inform staff, but through the transitional stages of changing the culture of a building to one of support such actions indicate the school's steadfast commitment to serving the mission and vision through structure improvement activities.

   ♦ Example: School Improvement Goal 4: Citizen High School will increase the percentage of freshmen who participate in extracurricular activities or clubs to 66% by the conclusion of the 2011–2012 school year. We currently have 62 out of 127 freshmen out for a fall activity. This is 48.8%. These data include football, cross-country, golf, soccer, volleyball, Student Council, Key Club, band, choir, and FFA. Other clubs do not know freshman numbers yet. Goal for the year is to have 84 freshmen participate in at least one activity.

2. An update of the entire plan should be the primary area of focus for each faculty meeting. This makes certain that the plan is a primary focus for building leaders and therefore they are continually updating and monitoring data as it is created. Just as data from assessment should be used formatively in the classroom, so should data collected throughout the year in regard to school improvement efforts. This monitoring and dissemination of information allows staff members to do their jobs to the best of their ability. *The collection and original analysis of data should be delegated as leadership is distributed among the faculty.* An example of a high-quality faculty meeting agenda (with subsequent minutes in red) is provided in Figure 2.6 (page 34).

Figure 2.6 SIP Goals and Progress

- 90% of the junior high students will score at a meets or exceeds level on the 2013 Illinois Standards Achievement Test (ISAT) reading test.
  - RtI interventions and routine progress monitoring continue.
  - Data meetings to take place on February 10.
  - ISAT testing is currently still the measure.
- Junior high students will score at a 95% meets or exceeds level on the 2012 state math test.
  - Alignment work continues.
  - State testing is currently still the measure.
- The attendance rate will improve to 95% for the 2012–2013 school year.
  - Still at 0.5% below goal. Push attendance! Where are the eighth graders?

Knight Junior High School
08/17/2012 to 02/02/2013 = 105 school days

Grade Level	Days Absent	Days Attended	ADA	ADA %
7	574.53	12775.47	121.67	95.70
8	753.00	11595.00	110.43	93.11
Subtotal	1327.53	24370.47	232.10	94.41 (average)

- Knight JHS will align 85% of core subject area curriculum to Common Core State Standards.
  - Please make sure maps are complete, August through May, for 2011–2012. Common Core State Standards that are explicitly being assessed should be attached to the curriculum map.
- Overall number of discipline referrals at Knight Junior High will decrease for 2011–2012 school year.
  - A call for the handbook committee to come soon.

3. Finally, all school improvement team members, department heads, and other faculty leaders should complete an audit of school improvement activities every nine weeks (see Figure 2.7). This structured distribution of ownership over the SIP

serves to promote the activities and enhance collective buy-in from the staff. To cause positive change, the feedback must be direct and frank; encouraging such communication from staff can serve to change the dynamic in a building from top-down to collaborative and problem-solving.

Figure 2.7 SIP Goals Quarterly Evaluation

Increase % of students meeting MAPs growth target by 5% for each area tested, or raise % to national average (whichever is higher) each of the next three years			
Percentage Goals for 2012–2013			
Grade	**Reading**	**Language Usage**	**Mathematics**
9th	51.8%	55.8%	61.3%
10th	50%	50%	50.8%
Action Plan Recap and Analysis			
Action plan step	**What has worked**	**How we are measuring success and failure**	**What hasn't worked/ What we will adapt for the future**
Curriculum mapping			
Common assessments			
ACT prep study hall			
Academic intervention days			
Data analysis training			
C+I Committee			
9th-grade team (middle-school model/common plan)			
Curriculum review days			

3

The Professionals

Define Expectations

Our environment, the world in which we live and work, is a mirror of our attitudes and expectations.

—Earl Nightingale

The quality of a school cannot exceed the quality of its teachers. Vision, ambitious standards, and commitment are starting points, but unless they affect teaching and learning in the classroom, they will not bring about significant change (Stewart, 2012). People make the choice to become principals or school leaders because they have a true conviction to make a positive difference for kids and communities. Transcendent principals understand that they can best make this difference by supporting the professionals in their school building. To provide the type of support necessary to cause meaningful growth, principals must deeply believe in their faculty and staff—not only in their competency, but also in their capacity and their personal desire to excel. *Successful principals believe so fervently in their teachers that they extend the teachers' belief in themselves.* Such belief is what allows great leaders to challenge their employees to continually improve and allows organizations to become excellent.

Great leaders expect excellence and articulate that expectation at every opportunity. This means face-to-face, via e-mail communication, at faculty meetings, through the school improvement process, and by always modeling the expected behavior. Teachers deserve to know precisely what the expectations are and to be supported in arriving at that end. Great principals want teachers to know the high standard they will be expected to reach because principals know that teachers want to live up to the expectations. Simply setting expectations will not transform a below-average school to an award-winning institution; however, communicating what the expectations are, why they exist, and how they will work can indeed aid in changing the culture of a school (see Figure 3.1). In general, follow these rules for defining expectations:

♦ Expectations are to be articulated proactively and with precision.
♦ All expectations should be accompanied by a rationale.
♦ All expectations and rationales should support the goals, vision, and mission of the organization.
♦ Expectations communicated should focus on what is important—that is, teaching and learning, not procedural issues.
♦ The answer "because it is in the employee handbook or union contract" should never be good enough.
♦ Things that are expected of the professionals must be important. What is important must be communicated consistently and in multiple formats.
♦ Building leaders should never violate one of their expectations of others.

Difficult Conversations

An unwillingness to have a difficult conversation is an unwillingness to lead.

Difficult conversations are a necessary, albeit unfortunate, part of life for a successful principal. There is a popular line of public service commercials that shows adolescents demonstrating various at-risk

Figure 3.1 Defining Expectations

Subject	Typical Explanation	Culture-Impacting Answer
Instructional time	Kids cannot line up at the door at the end of a class period to wait for the bell to ring.	Students should be from the beginning of a period to the end of the period. Saving three minutes of instructional time per day adds up to nearly two additional weeks of school.
Extra credit	We cannot have students earning more than 100 percent in a class.	Standards- or outcome-based instruction does not permit extra credit. If the work is important, it should be for a grade; if it is not important, students should not waste their time with it.
Dress code	We don't want to dress like the kids, but wearing jeans on Friday is OK.	We want to model professional behavior since our purpose is to promote positive citizenry; however, we also see the importance of students viewing educators as human so the occasional casual day is not only permitted but encouraged.
Social networking	Be careful—that is how some teachers lose their jobs.	Teachers should be active on social networking sites to keep abreast professionally. Interactions with kids and parents are to be kept professional. Thus, teachers are encouraged to keep two accounts on each site—one for personal use and one for professional use.

behaviors while their parents fail to confront them. The commercials are titled "Addicted to Enabling." Each time those commercials come on television, I think of the behavior of some of my fellow principals. Their sheer refusal to address behaviors that contradict organizational norms makes them no different from the parents in the commercials. By not addressing an issue, the principals are actually acting to promote its continuance. I cannot imagine anybody who truly enjoys partaking in these stressful and occasionally awkward interactions. Understanding when, why, and how to have them not only makes the process easier but also serves to change a school culture.

As was stated previously, two things great principals do are maximize the capacity of others and align the goals of the individual with those of the school. With that in mind, every interaction a leader has with a colleague throughout the day should be intentional. Each interaction should serve a purpose: to support the professionals in their own professional growth or to support their understanding of why working toward enacting the goals of the organization is so important. Throughout any given school day, the average principal walking through the building would need more fingers and toes to count the number of observed adult behaviors that do not align with individuals' professional growth plans or support the goals of the school. Each of those observances warrants a potentially difficult conversation.

Imagine your role as a coach to a young (pre-stardom) Michael Jordan, Celine Dion, or Tom Cruise. You sincerely believe that the person you are coaching has the capacity and potential to be truly amazing in the chosen field. You observe the youngster do something that is below his or her potential level, inhibiting to growth, or lazy—would you address it? When I have this discussion with other principals, the answer is almost always yes—and it should be. Great principals must view the capacity of their staff in the same light; to support and serve the professional growth of colleagues, such behaviors must be addressed.

Attempt to Create Self-Realization

The goal of each difficult conversation with your colleagues is self-realization. Once they are able to objectively evaluate their own performance, true growth can occur. This is precisely why video-taping and subsequently critiquing lessons is such a powerful method of professional development. Many certification, professional development, and recognition programs (such as National Board Certification) require teachers to videotape themselves. In my experience, teachers who have gone through the process of reviewing a recorded lesson believe it to be enormously successful because it mandates candid reflection and self-imposed critique. The critique is not adversarial—it is simply informative.

The lesson that building leaders should learn is clear. The more building leaders can expose teachers to factual evidence of what is taking place in the classroom (without judgmental critique), the more likely the observed teacher is to gain self-awareness. Through self-awareness comes the ability to improve performance. Leadership must be the vehicle to provide such information. Once observational information has been gathered, most often from classroom observation (which must occur in an impromptu fashion several times a semester), the feedback provided should attempt to provide a "videotaped experience" for teachers. Substantial factual detail should be provided to the teacher in a written debriefing, which should occur within 24 hours of the observation. This protocol allows the teacher to receive explicit feedback and forces opinions to be withheld until a face-to-face conversation takes place. Examples are provided below:

> **General Feedback:** The teacher did a great job of asking questions.

> **Explicit Feedback:** The teacher asked seven questions to students between 8:14 and 8:27, three of which were higher-order in nature.

General Feedback: The classroom was not well-managed during my stay.

Explicit Feedback: Between 3:12 and 3:31, six students left their seats without permission, one left the room, and the teacher "shushed" the classroom three times.

General Feedback: The purpose of the lesson was not clear.

Explicit Feedback: There were no written outcomes on the board, nor was there an agenda. During my 14 minutes in the classroom, the purpose was not directly mentioned, and when I inquired why students were doing the observed activity, zero of three could provide an answer.

The explicit feedback allows the observer (when following up with the teacher) to ask questions to gain an understanding of the teacher's perspective on the data provided. For example, a principal could follow up with a teacher after providing the information below in the following manner:

Explicit Feedback: There were no written outcomes on the board, nor was there an agenda. During my 14 minutes in the classroom, the purpose was not directly mentioned, and when I inquired why students were doing the observed activity, zero of three could provide an answer.

Follow-Up Questions (Face-to-Face): What reaction did you have to the written feedback? Did that reflection indicate anything to you about your professional practice? Is there anything that you believe needs attention in regard to professional growth as a result of reflecting upon the information provided? How can I support you through that process?

This process forces the teachers to reflect upon the data presented to them, much the way they would have to by watching a video of themselves. The ability to ask questions that allow teachers to come to realizations on their own provides helpful opportunities to support their professional growth. Providing data and asking for reflections, however, does not always lead to teacher ownership of the potential area for growth (at first). This may be frustrating; as a building leader, you may want to *tell* the teacher how to fix the problems. It is of the utmost importance to remember, however, that *true teacher growth occurs only when there is an internal recognition that practice needs to change.*

Explain and Attempt to Understand Why

If coaching conversations over an extended period of time do not lead to self-realization or the desire to improve, difficult conversations may have to occur. All people deserve two things in all difficult conversations:

- ♦ They deserve to be told why they need to improve on their current performance.
- ♦ They need an opportunity to explain why they are operating in their current modality.

The intent of these conversations is still to cause self-realization in the other party. The ability to cause a transformation in behavior as a result of self-realization is what separates principals who simply embody the role of a manager ("You did this wrong—fix it") from principals who function as leaders ("Why is this occurring? Let me show you a better way and why it works"). Imagine the scenario below:

> Erica Davis is a veteran art teacher with an extreme record. Her students have placed among the top five in the state art competition awarding excellence in painting and sculpture six of the last seven years, but she

has continually been reprimanded and even endured a teacher remediation for not being able to keep her class under control. Erica's principal, John Garza, is at a loss. He thinks Erica is a valuable employee and extremely valuable to kids, but he cannot allow her students to roam freely, talk back to her in class, and opt to simply sit out of lessons. Mr. Garza offers factual observation and ideas on how to improve the situation. When those ideas are not successful, he meets with Ms. Davis, tells her what is wrong, and suggests how to fix it. Ms. Davis still does not comply. Mr. Garza is beginning to feel personally insulted that his reprimands and personal pleas are not changing Ms. Davis's behavior. He also believes that Ms. Davis is truly sorry for these events when they occur and has worked to make the situation better. The areas that need remediation are simply not improving, however. Mr. Garza is left in a difficult predicament.

What Mr. Garza did in the above situation was identify a symptom. He did not provide the diagnosis from which a potential cure could come by asking "why" and explaining that he would be able to get to the root of the problem. When he finally asks the question "why" months later, Ms. Davis confesses that she simply dreads confrontation and fears losing her relationships with her students if she corrects their behavior. This fear supersedes her desire to implement best practices in her classroom. She is not unwilling to change, as her behavior indicates, but does not know where to start and is terrified of the outcome. With that knowledge, Mr. Garza is able to explain that while she fears damage to her teacher/student relationships, the current relationships are not healthy and do not support the school's goal to have a responsible, respectful student body. By asking and answering "why," Mr. Garza is able to remedy the issue, provide support, encourage growth, and reduce the stress both he and Ms. Davis were feeling.

Best Practices for Difficult Conversations

An unwillingness to engage in difficult conversations is an unwillingness to lead. Difficult conversations are just that—difficult. Engaging in a conversation that will knowingly bring angst or discomfort to the other party is stressful, but through discomfort *can* come growth. *The goal should not be to make the conversation easier, but to make it more effective.* There are a number of things that a school leader can do to potentially increase the productivity of difficult conversations—and potentially make them easier as well.

- ♦ **Have the meeting in the teacher's territory.** This tip has three distinct benefits: it provides additional security for the employee, allows privacy if the conversation leaves the employee emotional (no tearful walk through the office), and allows the leader to leave when the conversation is over.
- ♦ **Listen empathetically.** Put yourself in the other person's shoes. Everybody in the situation is human and has emotions. Try to understand the teacher's point of view.
- ♦ **Forget the small talk.** People do not want to talk about sports or the weather when they are about to hear some difficult news.
- ♦ **Tell only the truth.** Understand that attempting to make the other person feel better is truly an attempt to make you feel better. Be direct. Be concise. Be clear.
- ♦ **Be clear about your purpose.** Every difficult conversation is about one thing—supporting the other person's professional growth. This is true when a teacher frequently comes to school late, does not complete a word wall, or swears at a student. The intent of the follow-up conversation is to help that person become a better professional.
- ♦ **Use careful language.** Difficult conversations need to move beyond what the principal thinks or believes. State facts. For example, "Your professional practice is not acceptable."

◆ **Maintain transparency and follow up.** Do not say anything in a difficult meeting that you would not put into words and sign your name to. Stay professional and stay brief. Follow up the conversation with an e-mail recap that includes action items for all individuals concerned.

Lead Professional Development

Accountability must be a reciprocal process. For every increment of performance I demand from you, I have an equal responsibility to provide you with the capacity to meet the expectation. Likewise, for every investment you make in my skill and knowledge, I have a reciprocal responsibility to demonstrate some new increment in performance.

—*Richard Elmore*

Before you can hold a teacher accountable for a demanded behavior, you must first provide ample training to allow for potential success. Far too often people are put in very difficult positions with little possibility for success. This is the antithesis to being a servant leader to your staff. It is the leader's job to expect continuous growth and improvement, but it is also your job to facilitate that growth through support, training, and professional development (PD).

How to Encourage a Community of Growth

The only things that look the same in America today as they did in 1962 are schools. While the school calendar and buildings may look the same, leaders must work to make sure that the practices in schools are ever-changing and ever-growing. During an #edchat on Twitter recently, somebody tweeted, "As professionals, teachers should want to improve their practice on their own." I agree with the sentiment, but the operative word in the above Tweet is "should." For those who do not, it is the *responsibility* of leadership to engage them in their own professional development. This means that the building leader must serve as the instructional leader, instructional coach, and facilitator to all members of the staff. All new information regarding best practices, from technology to brain research to instructional strategies, should be consumed, filtered, and distributed in understandable nuggets for faculty members to address their personal areas for potential or needed growth. Administrators must serve as the lead learners in their building.

Activities to support the professional development of faculty or staff members may include the following:

- ◆ **Send out weekly best-practices e-mails:** Pick any best-practice topic and link four or five articles relating to the theme. These are not required reading, but if they are important enough to send out to people, they should also come up in discussion.

- ◆ **Assign faculty meeting readings:** Bogging down staff with required reading outside of the school day may be counterproductive, depending on the professional maturity of your staff. Carving out 15 minutes of a faculty meeting and asking professionals to read and have a debriefing about an article is entirely appropriate in all situations, however. Moreover, this indicates its importance. Faculty meetings are often considered the principal's time; your willingness to give up that time to promote best practices is a powerful indicator of what is important in your culture.

- ◆ **Create voluntary book blogs:** As lead learner you should constantly have a book you are working through. Sending an e-mail announcing a book read and setting up a blog literally will take about ten minutes of time and may engage 15 to 20 percent of your staff members in a worthwhile experience grounded in best practices.

- ◆ **Embed professional development in your school improvement action plan:** School improvement plans are collaboratively written and should largely focus upon student achievement. Since plans are designed to improve achievement, staff members must be given the training to change their actions in the desired manner. Thus, professional development that applies to all staff members should be embedded in the plan that drives school decision-making.

♦ **Model the behavior:** As the principal you should always model appropriate professional behavior. As the lead learner you should always be learning. Activities that foster your own professional growth (especially those that take place outside of the typical workday) set a clear tone that the status quo is not accepted and that continued growth is an expectation.

♦ **Use teacher evaluation data:** School-wide professional development activities should promote areas identified as weaknesses through personnel evaluation. Data should be recorded and trends regarding the faculty should be used to develop comprehensive professional development that serves the needs of the faculty as opposed to a simple "one-and-done" activity. Figure 3.2 is an example of a building-wide data chart—based on the Charlotte Danielson (1996) framework for teaching—that can be used to drive PD decisions. Areas of evaluation that appear in the "Unsatisfactory" or "Needs Improvement" columns with the highest frequency require the most immediate PD attention.

Identify an Individual's Areas for Improvement

To truly support teacher growth, a leader must take people from where they currently are at in terms of professional maturity and competency and move them forward. Just as the best teachers take information from assessments and differentiate instruction for students, so should the best principals differentiate their attention to serve the needs of their staff. What a new teacher needs and the most accomplished veteran needs within a building may be vastly different—or perhaps more similar than the principal might assume. Each person is different. Each person's learning and communication

Figure 3.2 Evaluation Data

Area of Evaluation	N/A	Unsatisfactory	Needs Improvement	Proficient	Distinguished
Demonstrating knowledge of content and pedagogy	0	0	4	22	9
Demonstrating knowledge of students	0	1	3	9	21
Setting instructional outcomes	0	0	4	13	17
Demonstrating knowledge of resources	0	0	1	22	11
Designing coherent instruction	0	1	3	23	7
Designing student assessment	0	1	4	22	7
Creating an environment of respect and rapport	0	0	4	14	15
Establishing a culture for learning	0	0	5	22	7
Managing classroom procedures	0	0	3	25	6
Managing student behavior	0	0	3	29	2
Organizing physical space	1	0	0	29	4
Communicating with students	0	0	4	24	6
Using questioning and discussion techniques	1	0	19	11	2
Engaging students in learning	2	1	4	21	6
Using assessment in instruction	0	1	3	23	7
Demonstrating flexibility and responsiveness	0	0	2	28	4
Maintaining accurate records	0	1	0	32	1
Communicating with families	0	0	5	24	5
Participating in a professional learning community	0	0	7	20	7
Growing and developing professionally	0	0	19	10	5
Demonstrating professionalism	0	1	1	28	4

style is different; thus, the leadership strategy employed in each situation should also be different. As a principal, you must adapt to the needs of your staff, not expect them to adapt to your communication or personality style.

To move the staff members (aide, custodian, or teacher) forward effectively and efficiently, a leader should use their individual performance evaluations as a guide. Each evaluation should serve as a personal professional development plan for the individual. Using evaluations to fuel PD allows the building leader to address the comprehensive needs of a faculty and staff through large-scale PD as described above, but also to zero in on the areas of potential growth for each individual as well. Figure 3.3 provides an example of a goal sheet to be completed collaboratively by evaluator and teacher.

Everybody Is a Leader (Shared Leadership)

> *There is a growing sense that effective organization change has its own dynamic, a process that cannot simply follow strategic shifts and that is longer and subtler than can be managed by any single leader. It is generated by the insights of many people trying to improve the whole, and it accumulates over [time].*

—*Charles Heskscher*

No principal will be at the same school forever. At some point, leadership will transfer. For organizations to thrive beyond the tenure of any one person requires tremendous effort from the outgoing leader to allow the change to create a sense of renewal for the school, community, and staff (Hebert, 2006). Organizations with healthy, supportive cultures have people ready and willing whenever an opportunity arises. A building leader performing at a truly distinguished level is actively developing leaders within the organization. This is simply an accelerated phase of maximizing the capacity of others within the organization. Truly accomplished

Figure 3.3 Goal Sheet

Personal Goals Related to Prior Evaluations and Informal Observations

Domain and component of Danielson model	Goal	How it can be measured	How can I support you to achieve that goal?	What PD can support you in achieving that goal?

Teacher Goals for Students

Goal	How it can be measured	How can I support you to achieve that goal?	What PD can support you in achieving that goal?

leaders focus on the creation of other leaders so that the organization can survive and prosper beyond any one person's tenure—including their own.

Delegation (Not Dumping) and Capacity-Building

When teachers observe administrators who are struggling, they often comment about how overwhelmed they appear. My personal experience validates this teacher observation. Many principals and school leaders have difficulty because they have so much on their plate and simply try to do too much.

Principals who are experiencing these struggles have often failed to master the delicate art of delegation. Many leaders view delegation as dumping—a simple way to make other people mad by making their jobs more difficult. Other leaders (those who over-value control) view delegation from a more personal point of view: delegation is simply a way for work to take longer to get done at a lower level than if they had done it themselves.

This may be the easiest change suggested in this book and one that will have the most profound impact on your professional career. Highly successful principals change their paradigm regarding delegation by adopting this construct: don't view dissemination of duties as delegation; view it as capacity-building. This phraseology forces a leader to think in terms of sustainability and distributed leadership. Every task in the school should be looked at through the lens of capacity-building. When the principal takes this approach, everything becomes a teachable moment. This changes normal, everyday tasks into opportunities for growth for others within your organization. This mind-set also prevents the leader from simply dumping extra work upon colleagues. It allows for every piece of work in an organization to be intentional. Simply put, it should become your goal as a leader that there is not a single thing you do for your organization in which you are the only person who has the expertise to complete the task at hand—this is true sustainability.

This process is grueling. In fact, this process can often become more time-consuming (at first) than simply completing the work on your own. Projects may need to be chunked, reports re-explained, and supervision duplicated, but this system of operation front-loads the work in a nonemergency setting. Spending two hours a week for one month working through the delegation process with a staff member may seem like an inefficient use of time on a job that would take you 30 minutes. However, the payback on your investment will soon be realized when that task is forever taken off your plate. The patience you exhibit during this period of growth for the other individual also demonstrates a true commitment to supporting the other individual's professional growth and to promoting true organizational sustainability.

There is no limit to what can be delegated or to the positive impact it can have on a school when the delegation of activities becomes viewed as true capacity-building. Figure 3.4 (page 56) provides a table of activities that many administrators spend too much time on and how they can be delegated and to whom.

Insulated Failures

The best support a principal can offer a faculty member is the ability to fail in a safe environment. This can take place in two very different scenarios: inside and outside of the classroom. The two situations are substantially different, but both allow for a leader to support and encourage tremendous professional growth.

American public education is under ever-increasing scrutiny, and despite the influx of research and technology, student achievement remains relatively stagnant. What has become clear is that continuing to employ the same practices and expecting different results is a recipe for disaster. As a building leader, you cannot allow this to happen in your school. Principals must empower teachers to take risks by creating environments in which they do not fear punitive observations and evaluations. Creating such a culture and providing formative influences will allow significant personal professional development of teachers, thus impacting student achievement.

In addition to establishing a supportive culture, leaders can promote innovation within the classroom in a variety of ways:

Figure 3.4 Time-Consuming Activities

Activity	Who Can Complete	How It Builds Capacity
Announcements	Students	Speaking is a standard. This is an essential skill for all 21st-century students.
SIP monitoring	Individual committees	Each committee sees the process through from start to finish.
Student handbook	Teachers, students, parents	There is community ownership over the handbook material, and different skills can be developed through the process.
Local Education Agency (LEA) at Individualized Education Plan (IEP) meetings	Teacher leaders	The representative serving as the LEA must view the IEP process from the perspective of the Board of Education (inclusive of the authorization of spending money).
Professional development activities	All staff	"The best way to learn something is to teach" (Frank Oppenheimer).
Routine discipline	Teacher leaders	Participants will view the discipline process from a different standpoint and gain a better understanding of the holistic nature of schools.
Scheduling	Department heads and clerical staff	Participants will learn a complex skill and gain an appreciation of how everything interrelates.
Website and social media upkeep	Students	This opportunity provides a leadership opportunity that is inclusive of an exposure to technology.

- Announce a new lesson of the month at faculty meetings or on the school website.
- Co-plan lessons with teachers based on best-practices articles recently reviewed.
- Model a new lesson for teachers.
- Require a lesson demonstration employing new techniques after a teacher has attended an outside professional development event.
- Send an "I want to catch you at your best" e-mail that encourages teachers to let you know when they are trying something new so you can stop by for an informal observation.

The second opportunity for insulated failure occurs when delegating an activity, otherwise known as capacity-building. This process works only when leaders fully comprehend that they are not transferring responsibility through this course of action; they are simply transferring the process and the workload. The leader still must own the responsibility or the system can crumble upon itself. This ownership allows a leader to coach somebody through situations of potential failure without negative repercussions. This activity builds capacity, character, and trust. Envision the scenario below:

> Dennis LaPointe, school principal, calls Bill Jackson, who has held his principal's certification for ten years, into the office. Mr. Jackson has shown capacity but has yet to embrace a leadership role in the school. The principal explains the potential he sees in the teacher and asks him to lead a committee selecting a textbook series by August 15. This is a duty that was given to the principal by the superintendent and is due on September 7 for the September 14 board of education meeting. Mr. Jackson accepts the responsibility and begins working on the project. The principal checks in often, but Mr. Jackson is having a hard time gaining

consensus among the faculty. The principal coaches him through many scenarios, but on August 10 Mr. Jackson states he does not think he can get the project done. Mr. LaPointe does not relieve Mr. Jackson of his duties, but begins to meet with him twice weekly and take an active role in the process. The process begins to take shape and on September 4 the proposal is complete and ready to be submitted to the superintendent. At the next board of education meeting, Mr. Jackson presents the plan and receives rare, public compliments from multiple board members—even a mention in the local paper.

This scenario reveals many lessons leaders should keep in mind when delegating that will help to shape the future of the school.

- Do not let initiatives given to others fail without giving the individual full and total support. If the only way that the project will be completed is to complete the task yourself, you are now a more informed leader. The task was beyond the person's capacity level at this given time.
- Take no credit and publicly give much. This builds trust and relationships with colleagues and hopefully their desire to continue to stretch themselves with such activities.
- The experience of working side by side with staff and modeling appropriate mind-set and behavior is always a positive way of working through the process.
- The principal gains a firm understanding of where the teacher stands in terms of capacity, willingness to work, and the future role that best fits the skills of the teacher.

Delegation viewed from the capacity-building paradigm is almost always a win-win situation.

Relationships

Nothing reinforces a professional relationship like enjoying success with someone.

—*Harold Ramis*

School Mission and Vision Should Come Before Relationships

School leaders need to be aware that staff members analyze the leader's relationships with an amazing intensity. Friendships between principals and teachers do occur—and it is quite possible that is healthy for both the individuals and the organization. However, leaders who want to support the professional growth of their staff must not play favorites or do anything that could give anybody the perception that they are playing favorites. Consider the following scenario:

> Sally Fitzpatrick, elementary principal, grew up with Ann Anderson and remained in contact with her throughout their adult lives. Three years ago, when Sally was named principal of Hawkington Elementary School in Montana, where Ann worked, Sally was excited that she would know someone on staff. Ms. Fitzpatrick and Ms. Anderson's friendship grows quickly as Sally becomes acquainted with her new town. Sally and Ann make plans before school begins in August to attend a live performance by one of their favorite comedians in early November.
>
> As the school year begins, Ms. Fitzpatrick finds that Ann is a very valuable staff member who runs many activities and is an active contributor to school improvement activities; however, she has some weaknesses in the classroom. One of the nonnegotiable items that Ms. Fitzpatrick announces at the first faculty meeting is that students are not to be sent into the hallway for any longer than five minutes before either being readmitted to

the classroom or sent to the office. Ann has a bad habit of not following this expectation. Ms. Fitzpatrick addresses this issue with Ann and attempts to explain why this is poor professional practice a handful of times in the early weeks of the school year. In October, Ms. Fitzpatrick takes a firm stance and advises Ann that this is not to occur again or her actions will lead to progressive discipline as outlined in the collective bargaining agreement.

Admirably, these interactions have not impeded the personal relationship of the two women. In addition, Ms. Anderson's behavior ceases after the direct conversation in October. Then, the day before the two are scheduled for their night out, it happens again. Ms. Fitzpatrick walks by Ms. Anderson's classroom and sees a student out in the hall. Ten minutes later, when Ms. Fitzpatrick heads back toward the office, the student is still standing there idly. Ms. Fitzpatrick is compelled to address this insubordinate act demonstrating poor professional practice by issuing a written warning in a meeting after school. Ms. Anderson responds professionally by apologizing for the behavior and acknowledging that it was contrary to what had been discussed and directed earlier, but also cancels their plans for the following night.

School leaders must show that enacting the vision and mission of the school is their primary purpose. When Ms. Fitzpatrick did so, her action ruined an evening's plans and potentially jeopardized a personal relationship. These seem like fairly severe consequences. Failure to put the school ahead of a personal relationship, however, can endanger productive relationships with the rest of your school employees. Moreover, this forfeits an opportunity to improve your friend's professional practice. Additionally, failure to act in accordance with previously established norms allows the school culture to be compromised for the personal (often temporary) gain of the building leader. This is antithetical to the greater purpose and thus contradicts the servant-leader mind-set.

In acknowledging the importance of relationships, it is also important for school leaders to acknowledge what they can control. Leaders can always be friendly, cordial, and genuine with their staff. Unfortunately, leaders cannot control whether they are friends with their staff—or how staff will perceive their message, as indicated in the example below:

MR. APPLE: I appreciate your coming in this afternoon; I will take only a few minutes of your time.

Ms. THOMAS: OK, what is going on?

MR. A: You have come in late three days during the past two weeks without calling to inform us ahead of time. This is unusual for you—is everything all right?

Ms. T: Well, no—I am in the early stages of a divorce.

MR. A: I empathize with the situation. Those circumstances can be extraordinarily difficult. Is there anything we can do to support you through the process?

Ms. T: No, not really.

MR. A: Given the situation, I am making the decision not to formally document this conversation, but I need you to realize that any further instances that violate our organizational norms will lead to documentation of the incidents and potentially lead to progressive discipline. Please remember that simply calling in to let us know you will be late drastically changes this nature of this conversation. Do you have any questions?

Ms. Thomas might leave this conversation thinking, "I am very fortunate to have an understanding principal," or she may think, "I cannot believe that my boss talked about potential discipline when I just told him I was going through a divorce—what a jerk." Given the staff member's perspective, both reactions are justifiable. Mr. Apple cannot control that reaction; he can only control his portion of the conversation. If he operated from the perspective of supporting the purpose of the school and supporting the professional growth of the teacher, then he acted appropriately in the above scenario. If Mr. Apple reacted by saying, "I don't care about your personal life—a start time is a start time," it would be hard to argue that he was establishing a culture of support for his employees. Leaders must remember that the vast majority of teachers want committed leadership that is firm, but fair and that provides a combination of support and accountability.

Tips for Building or Maintaining Beneficial Relationships

The people who work at a school are human. This simple fact is often what makes true school improvement so difficult. This simple fact is also what makes working in education so enjoyable. Leading school change means leading people. Great organizations become great because of the great people within them. Forming productive, trusting, and collegial relationships with staff members is necessary to create sustained change; however, doing so can be a difficult undertaking. Principals would be wise to keep the following tips in mind:

- Always strive to be friendly, not to make friends.
- Keep the primary purpose of the organization at the forefront as relationships develop.
- Understand that people are acutely aware of your relationships with others.
- Model professionalism at all times (even with friends), including via e-mail and while attending conferences.
- Remember that the only thing you can control in relationships with colleagues are your own actions.
- Be humane when you must deliver difficult news.
- Never lie. Speak using factual statements, not statements of belief.

Evaluation

The process violates everything we know about learning.

—Charlotte Danielson on administrator-
dominated evaluation

As the saying goes, teaching is the second-most private thing you will ever do. While amusing, that saying needs to be patently false in your building if you are to be an effective instructional leader. In the past, instructional leadership was viewed as a bonus when hiring a principal; today it is a role that all principals must occupy and great principals embrace.

The good news is that being an instructional leader has become easier in the past two decades. Previously, answering the question of what is good teaching could be difficult. The answer generally started with, "I believe." When operating from that standpoint of personal beliefs, it is difficult to provide critical feedback without sounding merely subjective and judgmental. Evaluation systems, tools, and methodologies were equally subjective and nonprescriptive concerning future professional growth.

This has begun to change. A rising consensus defining good teaching, based on research and data collection, has been reached. Frameworks have been created that allow principals to discuss best practices with confidence and guide professional development based on agreed-upon criteria explaining what good teaching is. Competing frameworks exist that you can consult, but all have the same core principles and serve to support the principal's ability to lead change in a building through rigorous personnel evaluation. These frameworks are being readily adapted into evaluation models in many districts—and even adopted by many states—throughout the country. Embrace this change as it occurs within your state or district. If it is not occurring, lead the transition.

Informal Observations

It is impossible to lead instruction without leading instructors. Great principals support the professionals in their buildings. It is impossible to lead instructors without spending a good deal of time in their classrooms learning about their professional practice. Failure to do so will undoubtedly result in evaluation being viewed as the arbitrary assigning of a rating and will not lead to sustained individual or school improvement. Observing a classroom and assigning the teacher's professional practice a summative rating based on viewing a single lesson does a disservice to the teacher, to the students, and to the school. Administrators must make time for frequent classroom observations if formative feedback is to be meaningful for both the evaluator and the evaluated.

Principals, however, need to understand that not all teachers are going to welcome administrators in their classrooms. If the presence of an administrator inside a classroom will be a change in common practice, the adjustment period will be uncomfortable. This discomfort is alleviated once teachers understand that the time that the principal spends in the classroom is for the purpose of supporting professional growth. The following guidelines for informal observations should be openly shared with faculty and staff:

- Informal observations will last 20 percent of the class or more.
- All informal observations will be followed by an e-mail noting what was observed, explaining how it related to the school's evaluation tool, and listing questions to reflect on for potential growth (see Figure 3.5).
- Feedback provided will be factual in nature; reflective questions are asked after each observation.
- Teachers will not receive more than one informal observation per week.
- All teachers will be observed for a minimum of eight times per year—nontenured teachers for 12—with no maximum number set.
- After every fourth informal observation, a face-to-face debriefing will be arranged.
- All comments will be linked to a segment of the agreed-upon evaluation framework.

Figure 3.5 Informal Observation Feedback

Observation Date	Comments	Evaluation Addressed	Reflective Questions
	TEACHER: SMITHSON		
07/25/2012	◆ Classroom had an aide ◆ When I entered, the teacher was working with same group of students the aide was ◆ Objectives were posted on the board ◆ Students were using data collected during a lab to hand write a lab report ◆ Most students could tell me what they were doing and explain the lab; a few could explain why what they were doing was important	Managing classroom procedures Communicating with students Engaging students in learning Using assessment in instruction	◆ How will you know if students really got the intended outcome of the lesson? ◆ Is it the best use of resources (time) to be working with the same group of students that the instructional aide is helping?

◆ Teachers who did not receive a formal evaluation throughout the year will have an end-of-year, goal-setting meeting for the next year based on the data gathered during informal observation.

Effective Feedback

No part of an administrator's job is as difficult as telling staff members that their professional practices need improvement or are unsatisfactory. Before teachers receive news of that nature, they should have received feedback multiple times to make them aware of areas of weakness accompanied by suggestions for improvement. When providing feedback to a teacher, a principal should thoughtfully analyze the information being provided. The following questions should be asked:

♦ Does the feedback support professional growth?
♦ Does the feedback convey the necessary message while being empathetic of the professional's stress level?
♦ Does the feedback explicitly identify and discourage the negative professional practices that were observed?
♦ Does the feedback provide the professional with concrete suggestions for improvement?

The intent of the feedback is to improve professional practice and create positive change. In some circumstances, suggestions for improvement and an attempt to hold a faculty member to a high level of professional practice are met with resistance or simply do not inspire the necessary change. In cases such as that, it is vital for school leaders to remember that their primary responsibility is to do whatever they can to provide extensive support in hopes that the teacher's professional practice will improve. It is an inconvenient truth, however, that some people are incapable or unwilling to be proficient teachers.

In cases such as that, one of the most important roles a leader can play is that of career counselor—to counsel that person out of this career. If someone's professional practice does not improve after exhaustive efforts, it becomes the role of the leader to remove that person from a position of influence and responsibility to students. This is undoubtedly the hardest part of being a school leader. These conversations are profoundly difficult, but when you have done your due diligence the decision can be made with a clear head and a clear conscience. This must become a reality in schools throughout the country if substantive change is going to take place. No amount of education reform will matter if leaders stand idly by and do not provide support and training to those who need to improve their professional practice, and subsequently hold them accountable if their performance does not improve.

Never let a temporary personal problem determine a permanent personnel decision. Personnel decisions should be made after considering the following questions:

- Is the person incompetent? If yes, dismiss.
- Is the person harmful or potentially harmful to kids? If yes, dismiss.
- Is the person insubordinate or unwilling to improve? If yes, dismiss.
- Does the person have the capacity to become a proficient professional although is not currently proficient? If yes, continue to support professional growth.
- Does the school have enough resources and time to work with the person to support that growth toward proficiency? If yes (*in successful schools, the answer is always yes*), retain.

4

The Students

Lead Instruction

He who rejects change is the architect of decay. The only human institution which rejects progress is the cemetery.

—*Harold Wilson*

The purpose of education is a topic that has been debated and written about for thousands of years, and finding a consensus definition is still impossible. My belief is that the words of Dr. Martin Luther King Jr. summarize the purpose of education best: "Education must enable a man (or woman) to become more efficient, to achieve with increasing facility the legitimate goals of his life." This definition is implied in the mission statements of schools throughout the country, as is evidenced below:

> The New Paltz Central School District exists for the children of the community. The focus of its programs and activities is the commitment to measured excellence and continuous growth and development for all.
>
> —*New Paltz Central School District,*
> *New Paltz, New York*

> To provide our students success in learning. We are dedicated to the individual development of attitudes, skills, knowledge, and responsibility essential to successful achievement in school and society. We actively

involve parents and the community in supporting student learning and development.

—Julian Unit School District, Julian, California

Provide a varied, comprehensive program that will stimulate students to become creative thinkers and problem solvers who strive to achieve their maximum potential.

—Dwight Grade School District, Dwight, Illinois

The role of the principal in working toward the enactment of the mission statement and thus the fulfillment of the purpose of education is complex. When boiled down to its core, it becomes clear that for the culture of a building to change, the adults within the building must become precisely focused on student needs; all actions within the building should be viewed from a learner-centered paradigm.

Define the Scope of Curriculum

Curriculum is an element of the job that is intimidating for many educators. The word itself can become intimidating because of its meandering usage in the everyday educational lexicon. Figure 4.1 can be used as a cheat-sheet guide toward understanding curriculum. Remember that it is not important that principals are able to recite the textbook definition of the following terms, but it is important to have functional knowledge of and be able to use the appropriate vernacular when communicating with your faculty and staff.

The concept of principal as instructional leader is not new. It has just changed from something that the best principals did to a role that all principals must occupy. While this proposition may seem overwhelming, all principals should take confidence from the fact that to be an instructional leader requires not a great depth of curricular knowledge, but rather the ability to lead people, analyze situations, and move the focus from the adults in the building to the students in the building.

Figure 4.1   Understanding Curriculum

Curriculum (plural "curricula")	What is intended to be learned by students—or planned learning. This is *not* simply a set of standards or a textbook series.
Instruction	How what is to be learned is taught.
Curriculum scope	A phrase used to refer to the depth and breadth of what is being taught in a given time period. Scope can exist for a lesson, unit, year, or entire K–12 experience.
Curriculum sequence	The order in which things will be taught.

The scenario below has happened in schools throughout the country in the past—and may still be occurring.

> Ms. Tilton and Mr. Guzman are both first-grade teachers who are well-liked in the community and have been teaching at Jostens Elementary School for the past 15 years. Sam Sawin, a mother of twins, asked that her children be separated in first grade to promote their independence. Sam's request was honored: her son Tom was assigned to Ms. Tilton's class and his twin, Kip, to Mr. Guzman's. When Tom and Kip began to bring home assignments and different projects, Sam, a teacher in a neighboring district, started to become concerned. The work the two students were doing was not even similar. Tom's teacher, Ms. Tilton, focused heavily on language arts while Mr. Guzman focused on science and math. Both students were making good progress in those specific areas but could not keep up with the other in the area not of primary focus within the classroom. This discrepancy sparked Sam to meet with the two teachers to see if perhaps the focus switched in the next semester and instruction would "even out" over

the next several months. The result of the meeting was disheartening for Sam; she understood that her twins would enter the second grade in vastly different places unless she made adjustments for them at home.

Principals must work collaboratively with their teachers to strictly define the scope of curriculum at each grade level, throughout the building, and throughout the district. Defining scope at the class, grade, school, and district level is referred to as curriculum alignment. Leading the alignment process does not require the principal to be an expert in any subject—the principal merely must be committed to the process and transfer understanding that the purpose of the work is to benefit students. Figure 4.2 provides a cheat sheet for understanding alignment.

It is the responsibility of a building leader to guide the faculty through the process of aligning the curriculum task. Creating a com-

Figure 4.2 Understanding Alignment

Curriculum alignment	This is a vague term that can mean many things.
Vertical curriculum alignment	What is expected to be learned from one grade level to the next (or logical course progression at the secondary level) is aligned. Gaps and redundancies are eliminated.
Horizontal curriculum alignment	All students in the same class (e.g., first grade, biology, calculus, fifth-grade choir) will be exposed to and have the opportunity to learn the same things—also referred to as a guaranteed curriculum
Standard alignment	What is being taught matches what is prescribed by an entity that has released standards on the subject. It is important when this term is used, however, to explicitly state what set of standards is being aligned to—remember that Common Core State Standards do not apply to every subject area.

mon curriculum presents an enduring problem; it is not a problem that you can solve in any completely satisfactory manner (Brophy, 1976). Without an aligned curriculum, however, it becomes nearly impossible to adequately support student learning.

The process of defining, refining, and adapting curriculum is circular and continuous. The role of the instructional leader is to promote and facilitate progress along an ongoing continuum (this process is never done). The most important role for a principal is to provide focus and time. The number one support a principal can provide is the opportunity for students to learn everything essential for them to know. This is not possible without an aligned, rigorous curriculum. To ensure that a school has an outstanding, aligned curriculum, the experts in the building (teachers, not administrators) need time to move through the process depicted in Figure 4.3 (page 76).

Define Learning Outcomes, Not Methods

Leadership must work with the teachers to align what every kid has the opportunity to learn. Each course and grade level within a school must have a defined set of outcomes, which students and teachers are mutually responsible for accomplishing. The teacher should have complete autonomy in *how* to teach what has been deemed essential; *what* must be taught must be common throughout the building. If this is a change in your building, you will face some resistance. The voice of the leader must be clear and strong to adequately support the students in the building. A school's having a common curriculum does not stifle the creativity of a teacher—the art of teaching lies in how material is presented. Student learning must be supported by guaranteeing that every student in a particular class has the opportunity to learn the same material that has been collaboratively deemed as essential.

How to Guide Collaboration During Curriculum Alignment

Part of the difficulty of aligning curriculum is that most leaders assume that collaboration is a skill their faculty already possesses. Collaboration is a skill that most professionals, including educators,

Figure 4.3   Aligned, Rigorous Curriculum

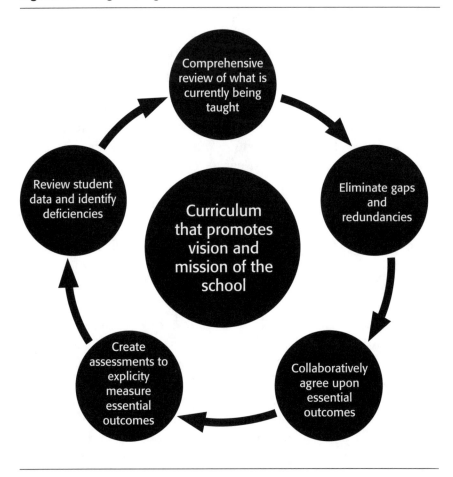

must learn. Unless school leaders teach teachers how to collaborate and establish norms, the overriding emotion in most teacher meetings is fear and the paradigm is adult-centered. Imagine the scenario below:

> Due to a shuffling of staff, an entirely new second-grade team, save one teacher, is established. One of the first charges of the newly constructed team is to agree upon a common curriculum based on a recently

released set of standards the state is adopting (sound familiar?). After analyzing the current curriculum and vetting it against the new standards, it becomes clear that Phillip, the only returning member of the team (and the team leader), should abandon his favorite unit (the snake unit) in order to better address the standards in a different area. While this is very clear to the others, it is not clear to Phillip, who insists on retaining the snake unit in the curriculum and suggests cuts of other, more valuable units. After considerable circular conversation, Anthony Schmerdla, another member of the group, suggests shortening the snake unit by 25 percent (four days) in order to fit in a unit better aligned to the new standards at the end of the year. This suggestion spurs more conversation, which eventually leads to consensus.

This metaphorical example manifests itself in many ways in meetings in schools. The teachers had good intentions and worked through a potentially difficult issue. However, the resolution they reached, as a result of poor collaboration, was adult-centered and focused on maintaining adult relationships and making adults feel valued as opposed to supporting student achievement and enacting the mission of the school. *Great principals do not allow collaboration to become the simple averaging of opinions or regression to the mean opinion.*

School leaders can promote collaboration and provide support to their teachers by establishing the following meeting norms and monitoring them for fidelity of implementation:

♦ A common purpose and objectives for the meeting must be established and articulated.
♦ All conversations must relate to the common purpose: supporting the mission and vision by supporting kids.
♦ Disallow belief or judgment statements.
♦ Data or research is to be valued when presented.

- Rule of five *whys*: any decision that is made should be scrutinized by asking five *why* questions. For instance, if the statement, "I believe we should eliminate the snake unit" (or the rain forest unit or any other unit deemed superfluous) is made by somebody in the group, it could be followed by these *whys*:
  - ◇ *"Why should the snake unit be eliminated?"*
    —"It should be eliminated because we have to fly through the material so quickly that it does not do the unit justice."
  - ◇ *"Why wouldn't we look to shorten the other units and provide the time necessary to teach the snake unit well?"*
    —"Doing so could possibly weaken the other units."
  - ◇ *"Why are those units off limits but the snake unit is not?"*
    —"It is not that they are off limits; this is just the quickest and easiest fix to our problem."
  - ◇ *"Why would we be concerned with what is quickest and easiest as opposed to what best covers the standards?"*
- The group should keep in mind—and, when necessary, discuss—that disagreements are professional, not personal.
- Once consensus is achieved and a decision has been made, it is to be supported by all members of the group.

Rigor

If one does not fail at times, then one has not challenged himself.

—*Ferdinand Porsche*

Over 40 years ago, Benjamin Bloom created a method to quantify critical thought (rigor). Since that time, Bloom's Taxonomy has been slightly altered (Bloom's modified or revised taxonomy), but educators throughout the world still agree that moving students along the taxonomy supports learning and student growth. Bloom's revised taxonomy chunks learning into six major levels, from simplest to most complex: remembering, understanding, applying, analyzing, evaluating, and creating (Overbaugh & Schultz, n.d.).

The levels can be thought of as degrees of difficulties. That is, lower-level thinking must be mastered before higher-level thinking. This progression along the taxonomy is now discussed as an increase in academic rigor. "Rigor" is a buzzword in educational literature, the blogosphere, and the professional development community and thus the concept of increasing rigor has become a focus of many schools—including mine. A rigorous, aligned curriculum taught with appropriate instructional strategies can impact student achievement like no other educational initiative—period.

Implementation

Changing the level of rigor in a classroom is more difficult than most people imagine. It is not simply changing the verb in front of objective statements and intended outcomes. For example, giving students an assignment to "create a map of Europe" by copying a map from page 52 of their textbooks is not more rigorous just because the verb *create* is linked to synthesis. Increasing rigor is about changing a teaching paradigm. Leaders must emphasize to their teachers that increasing rigor means challenging students to levels they most likely have not experienced, thus potentially causing discomfort. Any type of significant growth causes discomfort. Leaders must prepare teachers for this challenge and the initial kickback from students.

Rigor is necessary. Rigor does not mean more work; it means better work. Rigor means the teacher does less and the students do more. Supporting staff in leading them to increase rigor in a school should consist of the following:

♦ Define the term and be explicit. For me, the best explanation is Bloom's Taxonomy—others principals disagree. The important thing is not the specific definition chosen, but that all understand the construct and begin to implement it in their classes.

♦ Provide training. This can cost nothing: simply laminating pages of action words associated with each level of the taxonomy and creating a flip-chart can be of use.

♦ Caution faculty and staff that changing the wording of assignments (and not the methods of instruction) does not result in change.

♦ In order to cover class content in depth, there must be less content covered. This means that the mile-wide, inch-deep curriculum (generally textbook-driven) is no longer acceptable.

♦ Teach the students about rigor and why it is important to them.

♦ Monitor implementation and provide feedback.

Monitoring Progress

Nothing done to increase achievement in a school will matter unless it is monitored and formative feedback is provided—whether to students or staff. There are three major ways to assess levels of rigor in a classroom and to monitor growth: classroom observation, homework analysis, and assessment audits.

CLASSROOM OBSERVATIONS

There is no better way to understand the rigor level of a class than through personal observation. Changing vocabulary on lesson plans or outcome statements is much easier than truly increasing the rigor of a classroom. By experiencing the lesson firsthand through personal observation, a building leader can provide more detailed feedback to teachers to support the professional growth of the staff. A simple technique for monitoring the rigor of a classroom is to chart classroom questions and activities. It is important to remember that no matter how skilled a lecturer a teacher is, simply listening and/or taking notes is not a rigorous activity. A simple observation guide such as the one in Figure 4.4 can serve to monitor rigor quickly and accurately. This chart, when completed after an informal observation, would allow both the teacher and administrator to judge the rigor within a classroom.

Figure 4.4 Observation Guide

Teacher:	Observation Time:	Date:
Taxonomy Level	**Question Asked**	**Activity**
Remembering		
Understanding		
Applying		
Analyzing		
Evaluating		
Creating		

HOMEWORK

Homework is a hot-button topic throughout the country right now. Debates continue on how homework should be assigned and graded. This is an important conversation and one that all school leaders and faculties should have at some point. It still remains unclear (at best) if homework has any impact upon student achievement. One thing is clear: bad homework certainly does not improve student achievement. This fact needs to cause reflection about the design and use of homework (Dean, Hubbell, Pitler, & Stone, 2012).

Communication about homework design must include an analysis of rigor. There is a simple means of assessing homework practices: if the homework is able to be copied, it is not rigorous homework. Think about it—if I analyze a situation and you analyze a situation, could we possibly come up with the *exact* same answer? No, and the same holds true for questions that require evaluation or synthesis.

The only purpose "copy-able" homework serves is practice. If the homework can be copied, it does not require critical thought. Grading such work is nothing more than assigning an effort grade. Students should be graded on mastery of essential outcomes, not on attitude and effort—which are largely affected by parental involvement.

Leaders must engage teachers in this conversation well before setting into place any policies and philosophy statements regarding homework. A culture that focuses on supporting student growth will understand what role homework should play. If the culture is not healthy, simply trying to create a policy to create the change will not only cause tremendous debate and dissension, but will do little to foster or support professional growth or cultural change.

STUDENT ASSESSMENTS

Assessment quality is of extreme importance to sustain any school improvement effort. Remember that educational tests are employed to secure visible evidence from teachers so that teachers can make inferences about the unseen status of their students. Collecting data to support wise inferences is the essence of educational measurement (Popham, 2003). Great principals ensure that their staffs are not actively collecting and analyzing data from poor assessments. Leadership must ensure that the assessments from which data are being collected are of high quality and aligned to standard. Failure to do so does not support professionals as their hard work will not translate to increased student achievement (see Figure 4.5).

Principals need to ensure that curriculum is aligned, reviewed, and progressive (see Figure 4.6, page 84). The process begins and ends with establishing clear learning outcomes with matching assessments (scope), engaging learning experiences, and instruc-

Figure 4.5 Common Instruction and Assessment Cycle

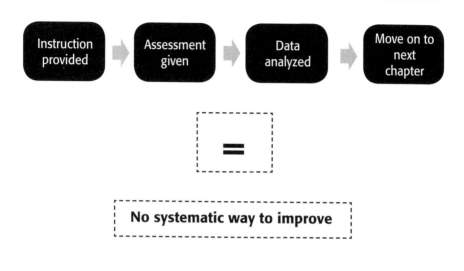

tional strategies (instruction) organized into sequenced units of study (sequence) that serve as both the detailed road map (curriculum) and the high-quality delivery system for ensuring that all students achieve the desired end (Ainsworth, 2011).

All assessments should be continually audited and compared to stated essential outcomes and the intended curriculum. Leaders can create an assessment audit tool, such as the one pictured in Figure 4.7 (page 85), to assist the process for their faculty. If assessments, outcomes, and stated curriculum are not aligned *and* questions are not rigorous in nature, all parts of the process need to be reviewed and potentially amended. The role of the principal is to facilitate professional growth in grade- or department-level leaders so that the thorough review of assessment is an ongoing process that is not dependent upon the efforts of administration.

Figure 4.6 Progressive Curriculum

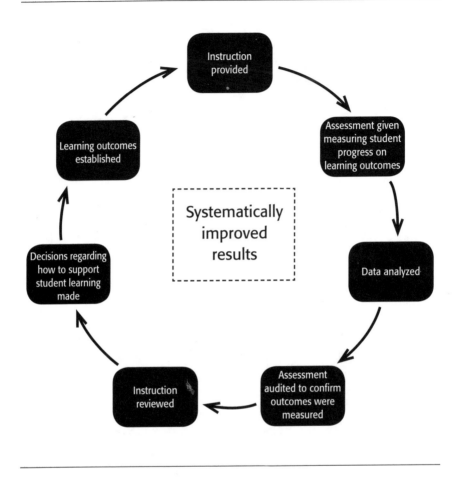

Figure 4.7   Assessment Objective Audit

Teacher	
Course	
Test Date	

Common Core State Standard(s) Assessed		
Objective	Identifier	Description
1		
2		
3		
4		

Other Specific Learning Outcomes Measured		
Objective	Identifier	Description
5		
6		
7		
8		

Question	Points	Rigor (1-6)	Obj (1-8)	Question	Points	Rigor (1-6)	Obj (1-8)	Question	Points	Rigor (1-6)	Obj (1-8)
1				16				31			
2				17				32			
3				18				33			
4				19				34			
5				20				35			
6				21				36			
7				22				37			
8				23				38			
9				24				39			
10				25				40			
11				26				41			
12				27				42			
13				28				43			
14				29				44			
15				30				45			

Reproduced with permission from Larsen, A. (2012). Oregon Community Unit School District 220.

Students' Social and Emotional Challenges

The philosophy of the school room in one generation will be the philosophy of government in the next.

—Abraham Lincoln

Consider the following scenario:

> Thomas lives in poverty and has very little support at home; however, he had demonstrated a great deal of academic capacity in kindergarten and on his entrance assessments at his new school. Thomas's first weeks at school do not go as planned. He frequently disrupts class by talking out of turn, getting up from his desk, and talking back to Ms. Rulz, his teacher. Ms. Rulz follows the handbook precisely and Thomas spends more time in the office than he does in the classroom. Gaining a quick reputation as a naughty kid, Thomas is not able to make the types of friends that parents would want their child to have. Instead, his peer group becomes the other students who are frequently in the office or the in-school suspension room. Thomas misses so much time in class, and the material is so substantially different from that in his previous school, that he becomes nervous and embarrassed in the classroom, continues to act out, and soon falls behind. As early as the mid-point of his first-grade year, it becomes apparent that his probability of success in school is quite low.

The actions of the school, while supportive of building policy, patently ignored what research has uncovered about understanding the behavior of students raised in poverty. Children raised in poverty rarely choose to behave outside of the norms set in traditional schools, but they are faced daily with overwhelming challenges and their brains have adapted to suboptimal conditions in ways that undermine good school performance (Jensen, 2009). All humans seek companionship and productive, meaningful relationships. Many students from low socioeconomic backgrounds do not have the benefit of such relationships at home and will seek to engage in meaningful relationships through school, often settling for whatever relationship they can find. A successful principal will find explicit means or programs to provide positive adult role models and relationships for such at-risk students. However, if the culture of the school does not encourage an adult to take that role, many times negative relationships grow as struggling students develop their own peer groups.

If educators and schools are to stop this cycle, improve student achievement, and change school culture, principals must foster atmospheres that embrace students of diverse needs and systematically provide appropriate modeling and mentorship. Educators must realize that kids are humans first and students second. The adults in a school must consider healing the souls of students as much a priority as addressing a vocabulary deficiency that will be exposed on the next state test. Social-emotional needs must be a significant portion of any Response to Intervention program in order to sustain success beyond the time of direct intervention. Great principals understand this need and program their schools accordingly.

There are some things a school simply cannot change about how a child has had to grow up, but educators do know they can make a difference. Understanding leaders can support this transformation by implementing a student-centered program as described below:

- Intervene as early as possible. While early intervention is a priority in terms of academics, it is an absolute must in terms of social-emotional support and mentoring. In high schools, make the conscious choice to exhaust available resources on ninth-grade students.
- Identify at-risk students prior to any transitional period by consulting data and risk factors and immediately provide peer and adult mentoring (this extends from kindergarten through senior year).
- Embed social and study skills into the curriculum. As much as it is every teacher's responsibility to teach reading, it is every

teacher's responsibility to provide guidance and support. This cannot be done without training and available resources.

♦ Creatively find time to provide additional support proactively while keeping in mind that at-risk students *deserve* exposure to the arts. Depriving students of time in noncore areas in order to address other deficiencies may not serve the mission of your district.

♦ Support an after-school tutoring program (with mentors) that provides transportation and positive opportunities. If a student must be pulled from art class to receive reading intervention, after-school tutoring provides another opportunity for exposure.

♦ Schedule student-led parent-teacher conferences as part of the curriculum. At-risk students need to learn how to take ownership of their education and be willing to self-advocate. This process facilitates both their growth and parent attendance at conferences.

A program embodying these principles at my current high school (550 students) resulted in the data displayed in Figure 4.8.

Figure 4.8 Ninth-Grade Student Failures

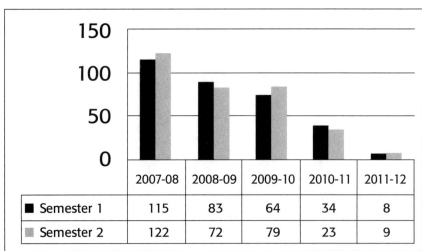

	2007-08	2008-09	2009-10	2010-11	2011-12
■ Semester 1	115	83	64	34	8
Semester 2	122	72	79	23	9

Learner-Focused Education

If paychecks were dependent upon student performance, the practice of learner-centered professionals would not need to change.

At the heart of the heroic journey in public education is the growing need to overcome the myriad student-centered challenges confronting schools and school systems today (Brown & Moffett, 1999). Every person (adult and student) in a school deserves to be known, valued, and inspired. The beauty of this phrase is its simplicity. The enactment of the phrase, however, proves to be very complex—a hero's work. A student who is known, valued, and inspired by classroom teachers is not a student who spends time in the office getting to know the principal, nor does the student ever have to struggle academically or social-emotionally without support.

Two Lenses

All educators, and especially principals, should view lessons through two lenses: one lens that is focused on the teacher and the instructional strategies, tools, and methodologies that are being implemented and another (more important) lens that is focused on the students and their reaction to what is being delivered to them. Regardless of how well a teacher performs when considered through the first lens, the lesson is not successful unless there is a corresponding message received when the lesson is viewed through the second lens. Thus, a lesson can be very effective or very ineffective depending on the student response. *Effective lessons are not determined by what the teacher teaches; they are determined by what the learner learns.*

The following questions should be asked to facilitate and monitor this paradigm shift:

- ◆ What do you teach?
  - ◇ Teacher-centered or content-centered (TC-CC) answer: Math
  - ◇ Learner-centered (LC) answer: Students

- What was the point of this lesson?
  - ◇ TC-CC answer: To talk about the Romans and their economy
  - ◇ LC answer: For students to be able to compare the Roman economy to our own

- How did the last unit go?
  - ◇ TC-CC answer: Pretty good—we stayed on pace and the field trip really enhanced what we normally do.
  - ◇ LC answer: Pretty good—91 percent of the students met standard and I have an idea of how to reach the other 9 percent to get them caught up.

- How are you handling the situation with Andrew in your class?
  - ◇ TC-CC answer: Since he has been absent so much, I am not sure he will be able to pass the class; my advice would be to drop him into a study hall.
  - ◇ LC answer: I have assigned him a study-buddy and developed a face-to-face method of assessment to measure his proficiency. If he is in school for the next four days, I will have him all caught up.

- At the end of the year, how will you measure your success?
  - ◇ TC-CC answer: If we covered all of the material and kids had exposure to all of the essential content, it was a great year.
  - ◇ LC answer: Through my student data and the students' proficiency in regard to standards assessed.

Being learner-centered naturally lends itself to best practices. This paradox between content- and responsibility-centered versus student-centered is the crux of many of the battles leaders face on a daily basis. *Influencing this paradigm is the most important work a principal can do because until this perspective changes, meaningful and sustained change in schools will not be possible.* Great principals lead their staff to a mutual understanding that the success of the adults in the building is dependent upon the learning of the students in the building.

Policy Alone Never Overrides Practice

Schools that are severely underperforming may benefit from having a leader who is simply an effective manager. This is why it is so much easier to go from being below average to above average or possibly good than it is to go from being a good school to a premier or elite school. To make the jump from good to better or best requires a true leader. A leader understands that simply instituting policy is not creating true change. A manager may institute the policy and the school may improve through this action, but no school can become great by simply having the right set of policies in place. Figure 4.9 shows several vogue policies, the intent, the reality, and how to align the two.

Figure 4.9 Policy Examples

Policy	Intent	Reality	Aligning Intent and Reality
Online grade books must be updated weekly.	Teachers will be able to provide valuable feedback to students in a timely manner and use data to inform any necessary instructional adaptations.	Teachers will most likely comply and update grade books. The intent, however, will not be realized.	Establish a learner-centered climate.
Our school will have a grading policy that allows homework to be worth only 10 percent of the grade.	Students will be graded based on what they know and are able to do in regard to the intended outcomes. Teachers should grade understanding, not behavior.	What was once homework will now be quizzes, in-class assignments, projects, or some other label that does not change practice, but complies with mandate.	Establish a learner-centered climate.
Our teachers will meet once a month to review data.	In a collaborative setting, the professionals in the building will be able to see trends in student performance and learn from each other in order to better meet the needs of students.	Whatever paperwork that needs to be done will be done. However, very little conversation about how it is apparent Mr. Johnson teaches the penguin unit better than Ms. Smith will occur.	Establish a learner-centered climate.

Figure 4.9 Policy Examples *(continued)*

Policy	Intent	Reality	Aligning Intent and Reality
Kids will get multiple opportunities on assessments.	Holding kids accountable to a standard and the importance of their achieving proficiency in that standard are not dependent upon time.	Individual teachers often have their own rules for students retaking tests. In most cases, students who do very poorly on an assessment and proactively come to the teacher to ask for help will be allowed to retake the exact same assessment for only half of the points. Thus, reality does not match the intent.	Establish a learner-centered climate.

In each of the above situations, the intent of the policy is altruistic and in line with best practices, but unless the school leader establishes a learner-centered culture, the policies will never have a profound impact on the school.

School leaders might also begin to articulate learning-centered principles of instruction to faculty and staff as building-blocks for creating such a culture throughout the building. The list below is not exhaustive, but it suggests the types of activities that indicate the focus is on the learner, not the teacher:

♦ Follow the five-minute-rule: the teacher should never speak for more than five consecutive minutes.

♦ Marking correct or incorrect answers on the assignment is NOT the end of the learning associated with a particular assignment.

♦ Use formative assessment in every unit in every class.

♦ Provide multiple opportunities for success on every assessment for every student.

♦ Allow student involvement in assessment creation. For instance, the teacher states, "These are things that you must know and be able to do as a result of learning this material—how can that best be assessed?"

- Flip the classroom: Transform from a dispenser of knowledge to a facilitator of learning.
- Use project-based learning strategies.
- Include enrichment and remediation in lesson planning.
- Provide multiple ways to measure student success on desired outcomes in each unit.

Classroom Management

The bad teacher's words fall on his pupils like harsh rain; the good teacher's, as gently as dew.

—*Talmud: Ta'anith*

A number of classrooms in schools throughout the country, elementary to secondary, rural to urban, are absolutely run by the students. Other classrooms *in the same school* are so well managed that students remain in their seats even when their teacher is forced to run out of the classroom as a result of some unforeseen event. Not every teacher whose kids stay seated have a world-class, research-based discipline system. Some may not even know about best-practice classroom management techniques. Four things keep classrooms in order and they all revolve around interpersonal relationships that focus on supporting the learner:

- Teacher ownership of the classroom
- An engaging class
- Clearly articulated expectations and norms
- Mutual respect

Teacher Ownership

Ineffective discipline systems absolve teachers from all responsibility. Consider the following typical scenario and identify what is missing:

Johnny misbehaves in Mr. Smith's class by letting an expletive slip while explaining something to the class.

Mr. Smith reprimands Johnny, but Johnny responds by saying, "Whatever— get over it, Mr. Smith, it's no big deal." Mr. Smith writes a referral to the principal's office and places it in Mr. Nelson's mailbox. Mr. Nelson receives the referral the next morning and calls Johnny to his office. Mr. Nelson and Johnny have a seven-minute conversation regarding the incident. Johnny apologizes to Mr. Nelson for his attitude and accepts his two days of detention as a punishment like an adult. On the following two days after school, Johnny reports to Mr. Andis's room to serve detention. Since only a handful of students are serving detention each night, Mr. Andis discusses the situation with Johnny for a minute and then they segue into a conversation about the ozone, and Mr. Andis discovers through the course of the conversation that Johnny is very interested in science.

What is missing? In this scenario (common in many schools), the teacher has no responsibility except to swipe the pen, establishes no norms for his classroom, defers to somebody else to make difficult decisions, and does nothing to gain influence or promote positive behaviors with the student.

Effective discipline programs emphasize prevention and require teachers to be involved and take responsibility in the process (Curwin & Mendler, 1988). Effective teachers build relationships with students and view involving administration as a failure in classroom management. A teacher with positive student relationships is generally able to proactively address whatever issue may lead to student discipline. To be an effective building leader, you address discipline in direct terms with teachers and provide support for them to take ownership of their classroom. In actuality, being direct and clear regarding expectations and providing the training necessary on how to truly support students through the discipline process is the best support a building leader can provide a teacher. Students deserve to have teachers who take ownership of their own classrooms and use discipline issues as teachable moments.

Engagement

A bored kid is a bad kid. Leaders, I encourage you to survey students to see which classes they believe to be the most challenging or most interesting. Then compile student discipline referrals per teacher and compare. (Obviously, keep the teacher names confidential and use the labels Teacher A, Teacher B, and so forth.) Without a doubt, the general trend will be that the two sets of data are inversely correlative: the more classroom rigor and engagement increase, the fewer discipline issues there are. The same results (most likely) will hold true in terms of attendance. This activity, especially when displayed in a visibly engaging manner, can instantly create a sense of urgency among your staff (see Figure 4.10).

Figure 4.10 Engagement Compared to Referrals

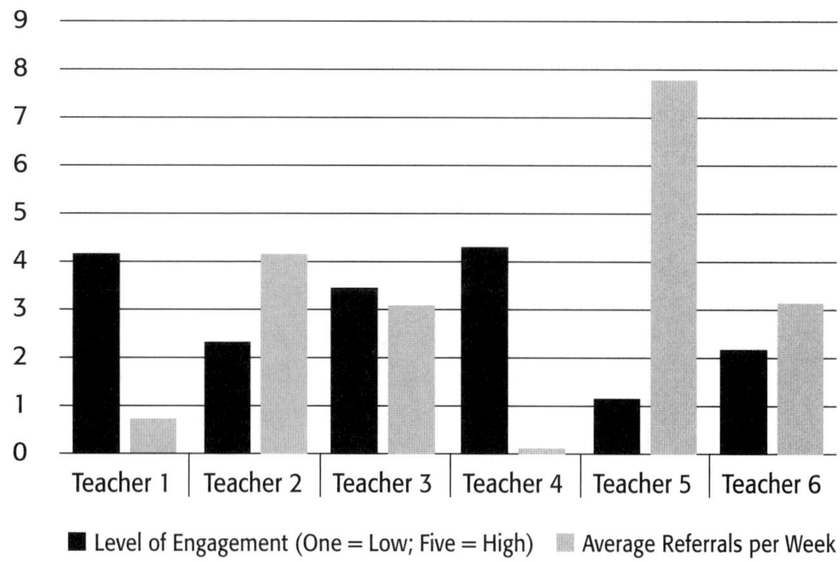

Level of Engagement (One = Low; Five = High)   Average Referrals per Week

This activity serves to transfer ownership of a problem perceived to be student-driven back to the adults in the building. Teachers can support students by owning their part of the process and problem, and leaders can support students by facilitating that transfer.

Clear Expectations

Just as teachers deserve clear expectations for their performance, so do students. Very productive and fond relationships can be built with firm expectations in place. Basketball coach Bobby Knight is a polarizing figure noted for throwing chairs and red-faced tirades directed at both players and officials. While Knight is not looked upon favorably by all, he is publicly adored by the vast majority of his former players. I personally do not endorse his leadership style and techniques, but it is inarguable that his unwavering commitment to holding his players accountable did not inhibit him from forming productive, lifelong bonds with many of them. Setting high expectations will not prohibit meaningful relationships, but on its own will not develop them. High expectations serve to support the development of productive relationships only when the expectations are enforced consistently and fairly for all involved. Great leaders collaboratively develop expectations that reflect the desired outcomes of the organization, school, or classroom.

Expectations are to be firm; consequences are to be malleable. Handbook-driven decision-making is the antithesis of student-supporting. Far too often students are told that the punishment they are receiving is based on what the handbook states. This implies to the student, and anybody else around, that the decision-making power is not in the hands of the adult involved in the particular situation. For all intents and purposes, the adult may as well be a computer into which the offense and student record are entered and which outputs a disciplinary sanction. Decisions that are handbook-driven as opposed to handbook-influenced operate in a manner that expels a seven-year-old for bringing a cap-gun to school because the school has a zero-tolerance policy regarding weapons. Leaders must work to make common sense and student-centered decision-making the focus of all components of the school environment.

Mutual Respect

There is a distinct difference between building rapport and show-ing respect and care. Rapport-building is asking a student athlete how many points she scored the night before. Respect and care are shown by pulling the same student into the hallway when she seems down in class and asking what is wrong—and not accepting "Nothing" as the answer. Rapport-building is something teachers do for their own benefit or the benefit of the class. Respecting and caring about a student is something that is done for the student. For a school leader, fostering a culture within the building that relent-lessly supports students—and their multiple needs—will serve to manifest a change in typical adult and child behaviors.

Intervention

A treatment method or an educational method that will work for one child may not work for another child. The one common denominator for all of the young children is that early intervention does work, and it seems to improve the prognosis.

—*Temple Grandin*

Response to Intervention (RtI) has been "around" for the past four decades, but within the past five years RtI has become an educational phenomenon. During this time, RtI has become one of the most dis-cussed, researched, and implemented educational improvement programs in the country. RtI soared to the forefront of education as a result of the brilliance of its conceptual basis. The philosophy behind RtI provides a rationale as to why it is simply not enough to cross your fingers and continue doing the same things that have always been done and expect different results with students who are struggling. "Hope" is a word that should not be uttered by edu-cational professionals when it comes to the progress of students. RtI embodies that same learner-centered focus that truly exceptional schools and educators embodied well before RtI became the subject matter of keynote presentations and consultant visits throughout the country.

The principal does not require a level of mastery in order to lead the implementation of an effective RtI program. Every school can have an effective RtI program. Every principal can lead this change in a school with any amount of resources. Creating an effective RtI program is about creating a fundamental change in beliefs and philosophy. I encourage building leaders to imagine their school as a vehicle and the core curriculum as its engine. The car may be beautiful, with chrome piping, beautiful rims, and a great sound system, but if the engine is faulty and dysfunctional, no matter what other repairs are done, the car will be mediocre at best and eventually fail. The same holds true for a school. If the core curriculum is not the primary focus of any RtI plan, the school may end up with many new interventions, but it will not create sustained, meaningful change. Adhering to the following core principles will allow any principal to lead the development of an effective RtI program that can create systematic and sustainable change for any school.

Focus on the Core Curriculum

Intervention, as defined through the RtI process, is a specific change in instruction to better meet the needs of a student. Intervention, in the manner most schools operate, is provided to a student as a supplement to or replacement of a current class. This process seems to make sense on the surface. If Billy Smith's data indicate he is achieving at a lower rate than his peers, he may be placed alongside them in sixth-grade math, but his teacher will also provide him with a software supplementation program during a period when other students are exposed to noncore curriculum. This practice works, however, only when the core curriculum and accompanying instructional pedagogy are strong. The assumption made in many schools is that they are, but current data seem to suggest otherwise. It is nonsensical to provide additional support to close the student's gap or deficiency only to return Billy to the original classroom where he will continue receiving poor instruction or below-average curriculum. When this occurs, the student will eventually regress and again need supplemental instruction. The first step to implementing a successful RtI program at any level is to ensure that the core curriculum is rigorous, aligned to standards, and common throughout the school (e.g., every third-grade student has the opportunity to learn the same material).

Embrace the Team Concept

Schools are beginning to embrace the team concept much more than in the past; however, the composition of a faculty team is often driven by any number of factors when it should be driven by one thing: having students in common. Teachers who share the same students during a given year should be teamed together. While any collaboration is positive, simply talking to each other—about adult-centered issues—is not the answer. Principals and teachers operating from a learner-centered paradigm understand that schools teach students, not subjects. For maximum impact, common teachers need to share common students. This becomes increasingly important as students progress through their schooling. Imagine this scenario:

> Brandon was a ninth-grade student at Highland High School who demonstrated enormous capacity at the beginning of the year and a keen interest in the social sciences. Through this interest, he formed a meaningful relationship with Mr. Osborne, a ninth-grade World History teacher. At the beginning of the second semester, Brandon's performance really began to falter and he shared with Mr. Osborne that his parents were going through a divorce and he was having a very difficult time. Although Brandon's grade slipped from a high A to a borderline B+ in Mr. Osborne's class after the first weeks of the semester, Mr. Osborne and Brandon agreed he was making good progress under the circumstances. Through the next few weeks of the quarter, Brandon maintained this grade level, and as the quarter came to

a close, Brandon seemed to turn a corner and was able to elevate his grade to an A-.

At Highland High School, all teachers received comprehensive reports for all of their students at the end of the quarter. Mr. Osborne was flabbergasted when he saw that Brandon had not passed a single one of his other classes. The next morning Mr. Osborne asked Brandon what had happened and Brandon told him he just did not feel comfortable opening up to the other teachers. Mr. Osborne then engaged the other teachers in conversation, asking what had happened with Brandon. They explained that he had shut down and when they had tried to approach him he had not offered them any information. After a few tries, he simply had been allowed to "check out."

During the nine weeks when an otherwise honor student was allowed to fail five classes, department meetings were held every two weeks to discuss common assessments and curricular issues. From all reports, the highly professional staff at Highland High made good use of this time and made curricular adjustments in order to improve their practice. The improved practice, however, did nothing to impact Brandon's struggles.

Now, imagine a different scenario:

Brandon was a ninth-grade student at Highland High School who demonstrated enormous capacity at the beginning of the year and a keen interest in the social sciences. Through this interest, he formed a meaningful relationship with Mr. Osborne, a ninth-grade World History teacher. At the beginning of the second semester, Brandon's performance really began to falter and he shared with Mr. Osborne that his parents were going through a divorce and he was having a very difficult time.

After class, Mr. Osborne immediately e-mailed Mr. Philrad, the ninth-grade team leader, to ask if Brandon could be added to the agenda for their common planning time later in the week. At Highland High School, the ninth-grade team was given common planning time and met at least once a week with an organized agenda to discuss solutions and innovative ideas to support students who were struggling. Brandon was added to the agenda for the following Thursday and the group discussed his situation at length. The team came up with a creative solution that included rearranging his schedule to include a guided study with Mr. Osborne and removing him from a difficult elective without penalty, encouraging him to make it up at a later date.

This change was implemented and Brandon was able to make it through a very rough year while maintaining a strong GPA and developed a strong bond with the ninth-grade team members as a result of their commitment to him and patience exhibited during his difficulties.

Proactive communication, a student-centered attitude, and intelligent changes were all facilitated by common meeting time revolving around students, not subject matter. Principals can support grouping teachers and promoting collaboration by scheduling to allow for the maximum impact of teamwork while not adding to the workload of teachers. Even in small schools with small budgets, leaders have enough flexibility in scheduling to make student-centered decisions that can truly impact student learning. Empowered teachers who are given an opportunity to collaborate and who care deeply about students will create a dramatic impact on the culture of a school in a very short period of time.

Catch Students Before They Fail

Educators have the ability to know which students may struggle to be successful well before the school doors open each fall. It is

Figure 4.11 Student Monitoring Chart

Student name	Incomplete/ missing homework	Organizational issues	Rough home life	Poor study skills	Poor social skills or decision-making	Other qualification (specify)	Total points
Adams, Samantha	Yes	No	Yes	Yes	No	No	3
Brightman, Katie	Yes	Yes	No	Yes	Yes		4
Carter, Marissa	No		?	Yes	Yes		2
Fitzgerald, Chris	Yes	Yes	No	Yes	Yes		4
Foster, Geoff	Yes	No	No	Yes	Yes	IEP dismissal/ needs support	4
Franklin, Scott	Yes	Yes	Yes	Yes	Yes	Retained last year in neighboring town	5
Greene, Alex	Yes	Yes	Yes	Yes	Yes	IEP dismissal/ needs support	6
Harris, Bret	Yes	Yes	No	Yes	Yes		4
Isaacson, Michelle	Yes	Yes	?	Yes	Yes		4
Jackson, Shannon	Yes	Yes	No	Yes	Yes	ADHD & needs support	5
Johnson, Chase	Yes	No	Yes	Yes	Yes		4
Jones, Todd	Yes	Yes	Yes	Yes	Yes		5
Matthews, Lori	Yes	No	No	Yes			2
Morris, Tim	No	Yes	No	Yes	Yes		3
Rice, Abby	Yes	?	?	Yes	?	Low ability/ may be retained	(3)
Richardson, Sarah	Yes	No	Yes	Yes	Yes	IEP dismissal/ needs support	5

Student name	Incomplete missing homework	Organizational issues	Rough home life	Poor study skills	Poor social skills or decision-making	Other qualification (specify)	Total points
Rogers, Samuel	Yes	No	Yes	Yes	Yes		4
Sanders, Benjamin	Yes	No	Yes	Yes	Yes	Was retained last year	5
Smith, Dustin	Yes	Yes	No	Yes		Needs support	4
Stone Martin	Yes	Yes	Yes	Yes	Yes		5
Thompson, Brianna	Yes	Yes	No	Yes	Yes		4
Trissler, Brandon	Yes	Yes	No	Yes	No		3
Williams, Teri	Yes	Yes	No	Yes	No	Likely to be retained	(3)

the responsibility of educational leaders to build relationships with feeder schools (and those schools that are fed into) to proactively identify kids who may need additional help and support. This process is time-consuming and will look different at nearly every level. While this task may represent an extra to-do on the lists of educators, there are no schools whose mission is just to have students be successful while at that school. The mission of all schools is to create successful, productive citizens, and in order to support the mission, schools need to operate in a proactive, collaborative manner with the schools they share children with. A simple chart fitting the needs of your school can organize data and provide a great deal of information identifying students who need intervention to best support success during transitional periods (see Figure 4.11).

Forget the Triangle

The RtI model will not maximize its impact for any school that has arbitrarily classified RtI as a triangle-shaped program with predetermined numbers in each tier. Proponents of the conventional three-tiered 80/15/5 system state that, according to research, 80 percent of kids should have their needs met by the core curriculum, 15 percent will need systematic supplemental support in addition to receiving the core curriculum in order to gain proficiency, and 5 percent will need a completely different program of instruction to be successful. However, this breakdown is not relevant or realistic for all schools and certainly not a strong enough statement to blindly base an entire program around. Some inner-city schools have less than 10 percent of their students meeting standards and others have well above 90 percent, so the 80/15/5 model works for neither. Rather than adopting some quick-fix program, exceptional principals work with teachers in a problem-solving mode to better meet the needs of *all* kids (Glatthorn, 2000).

In addition to arbitrarily chunking students based on what should be occurring, the standard triangle format neglects to include gifted students. In the traditional model there is no structure to systematically provide enrichment for those students whose needs cannot be met by the core curriculum. An effective RtI process is better described as a diamond with locally determined (and frequently changing) numbers in each section. This RtI model allows schools to provide a change in instruction for all kids whose needs are not met by the core curriculum—including gifted students. The concept of tiers within RtI is also self-defeating. Tiers imply a stagnant position, whereas a continuum implies continual movement and flexibility. RtI must be fluid.

The model in Figure 4.12 represents a fluid continuum of services that articulates the goal of servicing all students, including those whose needs extend beyond the core curriculum.

In adopting this model, principals must abandon the concept of any prepackaged RtI program as the root of school improvement. The staff of each school should focus time and energy on understanding the unique needs of its population and then providing enrichment and remediation activities to support learners whose needs are not satisfied by the core curriculum. An effective system creates opportunities that extend and reinforce the curriculum through local creativity and innovation. The ability to extend the curriculum can be maximized if school leaders place as much

Figure 4.12   Continuum of Services

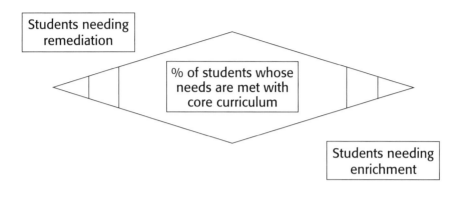

emphasis on meeting the needs of gifted learners as they do struggling learners. Schools can do so through enrichment activities which take advantage of everything from local partnerships to nationally established programs, such as:

♦ mentoring partnerships
♦ advanced placement/international baccalaureate/dual credit courses
♦ school-to-career class placements
♦ innovative scheduling opportunities such as entrepreneurship as a course of study or moving students between grades and levels to meet their needs
♦ online or technical opportunities (e.g., students serving as technology aids and troubleshooters in the building)
♦ programs to meet the talents of a group of students and the needs of the community (e.g., mural painting)

Social-Emotional Awareness and Support

To be successful, schools must serve the whole child. Students requiring intervention often are not only experiencing difficulty in academic achievement. The social-emotional component cannot be ignored if a school wants to create a first-class RtI model. Schools and districts, despite financially difficult times, continue to find money in budgets to hire interventionists, RtI coordinators, and data analysts. Yet very few schools are hiring additional counselors or social workers. This discrepancy speaks to a desire to raise test scores above all else. Many principals continue to ignore that students with social-emotional problems cannot maximize their capacity in terms of academic achievement, happiness, or future success. This concept, which is often ignored, literally goes all the way back to Maslow's hierarchy of needs and its impact on learning (Maslow, 1943).

The issue of social-emotional distress as a cause for needed intervention as compared to skill deficiency is amplified as students progress through schools. A typical 11th-grade student with a 2.7 GPA who suddenly begins failing three classes is undoubtedly facing some outside-of-school issue impacting her performance. It may be parental divorce, substance abuse, mental health issues, a traumatic romantic breakup, or one of any number of other factors, but it generally is in the realm of social and emotional health. Successful schools and successful leaders are the ones willing and able to dedicate the resources necessary to provide the needed support to the student. Great leaders and great schools value the needs of such students as much as those of a student in danger of not meeting state standards because of an apparent deficiency identified by standardized tests. Principals must know, value, and support all learners in their buildings. They must study local data and intervene with as much fervor for a student facing a social-emotional problem as for a student struggling with low academic achievement.

5

The Community

Schools Are Central to Community Pride

> *The trick to forgetting the big picture is to look at everything close up.*
>
> —*Chuck Palahniuk*

A school is an incredibly uniting community entity. The success or failure of a school has an extreme impact on the community surrounding it—and communities want their schools to succeed. Communities often view schools as museums of virtue, storehouses of memories, and prime sources of local pride (Deal & Peterson, 1999). Communities are hungry for the success of the institution that helps them raise their children and truly want to be supportive of their leaders.

It can be very easy for a principal to forget that the vast majority of people in the community truly want you to succeed. There are days and months when it seems that everybody who walks through the door has a complaint or a problem needing prompt attention. Principals must remember that community members usually express concern for the operations of a school for one of two reasons: either to protect a personal interest and/or as a result of legitimate concern for the well-being of the school. Frequently, leaders respond to criticism or concerns raised about the performance of a school in a very political manner. More often than not, the leader acts to pacify the complainant, defend or rationalize the occurrence, and move forward as quickly as possible. This method of operation ignores the fact that each nugget of information a leader gains has the potential to be valuable because people from outside can often see that which people inside cannot.

Instead of acting defensive or dismissive, the principal should take all complaints seriously and document them (see Figure 5.1).

Figure 5.1 Complaints Form

FILL OUT ALL AREAS FOR ALL COMPLAINTS
Date:
Time:
Parent name and preferred contact method:
Stated issue:
Next action: (circle one)
Refer parent to teacher   Provide concrete answer
Will look into further
Organizational issue or norm potentially involved:
Did additional information indicate issue needed public attention / private attention /both/neither?
How can behavior aligned with organizational norms and behavior supportive of the school's mission be promoted?

This process formalizes taking outside input seriously. It allows you to analyze information, such as "students feel like they are visitors in their own school" or "there is no personal connection between the adults in the building and students," that cannot be expressed through a spreadsheet. All complaints, notifications, and communication should be viewed from the paradigm that this community member truly wants the school to be great and that is why the person is in your office, on the phone, or sending an e-mail right now. Every voiced community concern is an opportunity to truly improve your school and/or to restore or promote community pride in your school.

Bad Reports Travel Far

Community members have a unique perspective on a school that cannot, and should not, be ignored. Many times, the sources of community unrest are the reports they receive from the people closest to the situation: the students. This makes the information extremely relevant but not always timely. Imagine the scenario below:

> Peggy and Rich Scott have lived in Pleasantville, Minnesota, their entire lives. In fact, they are the fourth generation of Scotts to have lived in this area. Rich is a chiropractor in town and president of the local Rotary Club; Peggy is a real estate agent. Peggy and John have four children, ages 24, 22, 21, and 11. Their second son, the 22-year-old, had a difficult high school experience. He was a victim of sports-team hazing as a freshman, which understandably altered his perception of the school and his academic performance. When the Scotts approached the administration with their concern for their son's situation, they were essentially told, "Boys will be boys." Since then, the Scotts have openly talked of the situation and their more than modest level of disdain for Pleasantville High School with friends, customers, and other community members.
>
> Many other community members were left with similar impressions of Pleasantville High, and as a result, the administration was turned over after the Scott family's third child graduated. A new principal, Mr. Elway, was hired the next summer and the school has changed. Test

scores have gone up, parents and students are happy, and a complete audit of athletic department activities has taken place.

Unfortunately, the Scotts have no children currently in the high school (and will not for some time) and neither does anyone in their group of friends. While many great things have happened at the school, very few have been media-worthy and the school outreach to the community has been secondary to fixing the actual problems within the school. The Scotts and other families of similar opinion without children in school are not aware of this positive shift. Therefore, their negative image of the school is still being broadcast quite frequently to patients, customers, community members, and even potential homeowners.

Changing school culture is difficult, and although it can happen rapidly, the public perceptions of a school, a department, a grade level, or even a teacher may take several years and several cycles of students to change. The good news is that public perceptions are ductile and great leaders can turn around community images of schools with concentrated efforts to improve school-community relations and a relentless pursuit of positive information dissemination.

The more populated an area a school serves, the more difficult it becomes to receive media attention. School leaders in population-dense areas need to be even more relentless in promoting their successes. In major metropolitan areas, weeks can go by without a single positive mention of the activities taking place in schools. In that time, hundreds of positive events will have occurred. All principals need to make a conscious effort to disseminate that information in multiple formats, including school websites and social media, and there should also be a weekly commitment to sending out at least one press release. You should have at least one item (not relating to any particular sporting event) to promote within the community each week. Ideas for weekly press releases include the following:

- Breakdown of meaningful data in an easy-to-digest manner
- Reporting of outside student recognition
- Explanation of service activities
- Student profiles
- Teacher profiles
- Lesson of the week
- Department of the month

This activity does not need to be a time drain on the organization. Press relations can be used as a capacity-building activity for an aspiring building leader, assigned as a class project, or even made the responsibility of a small group of student leaders.

The Five S's

Schools can create names for themselves and attract people in five ways, which can be labeled the five S's: sports, student achievement, specials, safety, and service. Dramatic success in any of these five areas can have a significant impact on a school's reputation and community pride. As is true, with everything associated with a school, the principal can play a vital role in facilitating positive performance in each area and positive promotion of the performance.

Sports

Sports have the ability to raise community pride more quickly and possibly in more ways than any other program within a school. For better or for worse, sports are the most visible part of a school. The success of students, coaches, and programs are immediately known and discussed on a weekly basis in the community. The data from sports competitions are broadcast on local newscasts, in the paper, and via the Internet. A high-achieving sports program can do in one year what it might take any other program decades to do: change a reputation.

In addition, sporting events are often the best-attended school functions, sometimes outdrawing even graduation. People often pay to enter sporting events, which brings revenue not only to the school through proceeds from the gate and concession stands, but also to the community. During one weekend of sporting events at my school (enrollment 550), over 1,000 students participated in activities ranging from soccer to cross country to volleyball to football. The amount of revenue such events create is dramatic for a town as many people eat, shop, fuel up, and take part in any other number of activities while in the area. Sports also provide a needed distraction in some areas, improving morale and in some cases even reducing crime throughout an entire community. If everybody in town is at the basketball game, it is easy to promote positive behaviors as opposed to monitoring negative ones.

STUDENT ACHIEVEMENT

Students' academic success may have the most powerful influence on school–community relations, but it takes significantly longer to change community perspective through student achievement than almost any other of the five S's. The excruciatingly slow release of data and the manner in which the media cover school and student data allow both positive and negative reputations to last too long. However, perceptions do change. A commitment to progress, opportunity, and high expectations will allow a school to determine its own reputation in due time.

By listening to community feedback and directing improvement efforts of a school to match the needs of the community, a groundswell of support can happen quickly. In some areas this may mean an expansion of advanced opportunities for students, including a gifted program at the elementary level and advanced courses at the secondary level. In other areas it may mean providing courses of study that match employment needs in the area—through medical training, agriculture education, welding field experience, or any other of a litany of possibilities. A commitment to progress, opportunity, and high expectations allows a school to determine its own reputation in due time.

All parents want their children to attend great schools. In the polarizing movie *Waiting for "Superman,"* this concept was explored in a very emotional manner, condemning public schools in some urban areas. Whether or not one believes that movie was biased, it is inarguable that most parents care deeply and value their children's education. As a principal, you want students in your school whose parents care deeply about their education. Thus, making your school an attractive choice to people that have the ability to choose where to send their children is part of your job responsibility. Positive press, pamphlets and flyers designed specifically for real estate agencies, and signage throughout a community can attract more parents to your school.

SPECIALS

A great band, choir, language, or drama department can have the same galvanizing impact on a community that a successful sports program can. In some communities, the school play or musical is sold out months before the curtain rises, and that type of positive exposure for students and the school is hard to match. Given the current economic times, one of the first areas to be cut from schools is specials. As such programs continue to be eliminated in some schools, maintaining or creating a strong tradition does a tremendous amount to build community pride in a school.

Special services can also attract students and parents. This can refer to special education services or unique programs offered only in one school. Special education expertise and location of services can certainly impact (both positively and negatively) parents' willingness to send their children to a given school. A school that can offer comprehensive care for students would undoubtedly be more attractive than a school that only does what is legally required.

The more offerings provided to students, the more a school can maximize their capacity. Schools can attract students through successful programming in the arts, languages, elective offerings, and access to rigorous courses. Students benefit from attending a primary school that offers music and art at each grade level, as opposed to schools that have cut those programs. Parents see tremendous value in sending their children to a high school that offers opportunities to earn 40 college credits for advanced courses, as opposed to a school where students can earn only 10 college credits. Specials can also gain attractiveness based on the esteem in which particular teachers are held. A well-known band or choir director can attract students from throughout the state to a given high school. Success breeds success.

Safety

Student safety and discipline are hot-button topics that draw significant press attention and also can be very quickly blown out of proportion. Earning a reputation as a safe, drug-free school is hard work, and that status may be among the most fragile to keep in place, but the most valuable to have.

In certain locations, safety and student discipline concerns trump all other parental considerations. That being said, it would be a rare school that could claim greater student safety than its neighbors without exceeding their output in other areas as well. Safety within a school may have an impact on enrollment, but generally in a negative sense. Students who do not feel safe will often choose not to attend a particular school and if moving is not an option, then not attending any school may be the response from an adolescent. High mobility rates and low graduation rates not only deter a school's effort to attract students, but also may lead to students' voluntarily leaving or avoiding attending the school.

Service

A school's commitment to community service can quickly and dramatically change public perception. Creating the mindset among faculty, staff, and students that the school needs to support the community as much as the community needs to support the school quickly creates meaningful partnerships. Once a community realizes that a school wants to help the area succeed, many past transgressions can be forgiven. In addition, tying the students to the community in a proactive manner encourages alumni to raise their own families in the area.

The Principal's Role in the Five S's

Schools serve their communities by being successful. Schools are successful when leadership fosters a culture of support within the school by focusing on the mission and vision and serving the development of the people (professionals and students) in the building. Once the culture of a school embodies that kind of support, some of the five S's will take place naturally. The large hurdle for the principal is to use programming and past experience to change the paradigm, moving students from expecting their community to provide for and support them to finding ways to provide for and support their community. Figure 5.2 shows a sample to-do list to help principals jumpstart their support of the five Ss.

Figure 5.2   To Do List: The Five S's

Sports: ☐ Evaluate coaches on how their performance aligns to mission and vision—not just wins and losses. ☐ Accentuate the positive (banners, t-shirts, announcements) to create a sense of pride. ☐ Promote data linking athletic activity to increased academic achievement.
Student Achievement: ☐ Promote the positive. Ensure the community knows about more than just one standardized test score. ☐ Promote individual student successes as school successes. ☐ Focus on the students. Make sure they know they attend a great school. (Student pride in the school filters quickly through a community.)
Specials: ☐ Focus on making the school great at one thing, as opposed to average in many things. ☐ Pay attention to all activities. As principal, it is as important to attend a band concert and a math competition as the Friday night football game. ☐ Protect non-core areas that benefit students when creating the schedule.
Safety: ☐ An unsafe school cannot have a healthy culture. Make creating or maintaining a safe environment a priority. ☐ Reward positive behaviors in age-appropriate fashion. ☐ Create a solution-finding/innovation team (commonly called a problem-solving team) to address concerns of groups or individuals.
Service: ☐ Create a program to track student service hours. ☐ Incentivize the program by creating tiers or thresholds for awards (for example, a student must complete 800 hours of service to be eligible for a particular scholarship). ☐ Promote the program within the community and use social media to seek out community service opportunities.

Communication

> *The single biggest problem in communication is the illusion that it has taken place.*
>
> *—George Bernard Shaw*

Everybody has a different preferred method of communication: what is effective for one person or group of people will not be for another. Communication is not an exact science. Schools and leaders often communicate in the modality that they are most comfortable with and expect others to adapt. Highly effective leaders find the modality that their audiences use, even if it means stretching themselves out of their own comfort zone. In my current school, for example, Facebook is a better avenue for promoting school and community service events than Twitter, the school webpage, or daily announcements when it comes to communicating with students. This may change annually given the nature of social media and Internet access, so as a leader it is your job to keep track of the tech habits of your stakeholders.

Establish Rules at the Beginning

Organizational norms and expectations must be set and communicated to students and parents throughout their experience with the school. As the parents of a kindergarten student this year, my wife and I were immediately informed that his "red folder" needed to be checked each night and returned to school each morning. We also learned the proper school door to be used if our son was to leave school early and the correct way in which to send his lunch money to school, among many other things. This level of specific, accurate, thorough information is characteristic of a school that communicates effectively. The flipside is a school that communicates erratically; for example, in August a student's hot lunch menu is e-mailed home, in September it is posted on the website, and in October it is sent home and posted to the website. If this were the case, the parents would have no idea what to expect in November. Leaders who are good communicators are systematic and methodical with their messages and resist the urge to overcommunicate and fall into such a pattern described above.

A simple addition to the student handbook and a separate hand-out at registration can alleviate parents' angst about their children's school routines by supplying the following essential information:

◆ All emergency notifications (school closings, etc.) will be broadcast through the school's alert messaging system.
◆ Reminders for all early dismissals, late starts, and no-school days will also be broadcast via the alert messaging system.
◆ Daily announcements will always be posted on the school website.
◆ School lunch menus will be sent home with each child on the last Friday of the month.
◆ All important information will be taken from the daily announcements and tweeted with account @sampleschoolannouncements.
◆ All service opportunities will be posted on the Sample School Service Facebook page.
◆ All district sports results will be available on the school website and broadcast via Twitter @sampleschoolathleticdepartment.

Providing a clear roadmap for parents and students to follow also gives clarity to all other departments within a school, schools in the district and the area, as well the local media agencies. The direct publication of such information also serves as an accountability measure for the professionals within the school regarding the expectations for communication. Systematizing this process allows school and community communication to become routine, proactive, and sustainable.

Be Consistent

Is overcommunication possible?

Yes and no. It is not possible if you are communicating in the right manner. More than one phone call regarding a particular non-emergency event or notice from a school, when not requested, can be bothersome for a parent. However, communicating in all possible modalities, and constantly communicating in modalities that are not invasive, will not aggravate stakeholders. Communicating via a website, social media, posted flyers, or any other source that does not necessarily reach out to the audience, but instead requires the audience to seek out the information, will not be regarded as annoying. This is the beauty of social media and websites for schools. Parents, students, and community members always have the option to opt out or ignore non-essential information through social media, school websites, and press releases. Vital information, however, should be conveyed directly (e.g., via phone, letters, e-mail), but should occur less frequently. A quick guide is provided in Figure 5.3.

Figure 5.3 Communication Types

Perceived as invasive communication: use only once per given event	Perceived as optional communication: constantly repeat
♦ Generic phone messages ♦ Letters home ♦ Personal contact	♦ Social media (Twitter, Facebook) ♦ School websites ♦ Press releases

Community Support

A school, and especially the principal's office, can be a scary place for some parents. Traumatic, sometimes life-changing moments have happened for many people when sitting across the desk from a school leader. Research has informed us that parents who did poorly in school themselves may have a negative attitude about their children's schools (Freiberg, 1993). Leaders need to be aware that the perceptions of school leadership for many parents can be centered on their own past experiences, not those of their children. Understanding that, and then moving on to ensure that similar negative experiences are not happening in schools today, while proactively putting effort into mending the damaged relationships that already exist, is essential if a principal is to engage a hesitant community.

Many community members fear schools because of a sense of personal inadequacy. Most parents want to do what is best for their children, but struggle to know what that means. Even teachers may not know how to best serve their students' needs. Many secondary educators struggle with teaching their own children how to read, and many primary educators are lost when it comes to helping their own children with physics homework. I personally had to ask my son's future teacher for help in finding and teaching sight words because I did not know the best way. The difference is that educators often have the connections and ability to send an e-mail to one teacher and be provided with best-practice advice. Not every parent is so fortunate. Great principals know and respond to this potential problem by identifying the needs of the local area and creating systems to better support the community.

Identify Community Needs

Effective school leaders work to provide a variety of services for their community members, parents, and future students. Great principals decide that they are proactively going to engage the community and support the citizens in their community. By offering workshops, outreach, support groups, and other educational supports, the school will reap multiple benefits from singular activities. These activities can be as simple as getting lists of sight words into the hands of pre-K parents or providing workshops on how to best provide discipline for a three-year-old. Ultimately, the time spent working with parents will benefit the future students. It will also allow parents to gain a greater level of comfort interacting with the school. This comfort coupled with the sentiment that the school has provided them with a truly useful skill will help build productive community relationships.

Working to bridge the gaps with those who did not enjoy their school experience does not need to be put off until they have children. A school can provide services that are needed in the community and transform the school into a safe and fun place for those who once had a less than ideal experience. Below is a brief list of some of the numerous things schools can do to fulfill a need in their community:

♦ Host community college courses.
♦ Create public hours for school computer labs.
♦ Allow for supervised open gyms for the public.
♦ Offer parenting courses.
♦ Offer workshops on hot topics in education.
♦ Offer informational evenings on complex issues
  (e.g., Free Application for Federal Student Aid, tax returns).
♦ Provide day-care facilities.
♦ Offer foreign language programming.
♦ Offer GED support.
♦ Offer access to technology.

A principal who invites visitors into the school in nonthreatening situations (school-related or non-school-related) and ensures they have a positive experience will be more likely to influence their opinions regarding the school than a leader who idly sits waiting for a community member's child to attend the school.

Planning School-Community Programs and Services

From Los Angeles to San Antonio to Mayberry, every community has power brokers and other people who carry significant political clout and influence. Generally, there are a few groups or activities in which these people congregate and enjoy fellowship. In some communities this is the Chamber of Commerce, in others the Lions or the Rotary, and in others a church or other religious group. These organizations often have tremendous power. The choice of the next mayoral candidate, school board president, or alderman may be informally decided upon during these meetings.

These are the people whom school leaders should be fighting to get in front of to discuss their schools. Every school leader should identify the three major groups comprising the most power brokers in the community and proactively schedule speaking appearances annually. Doing so is a tremendous strategy to engage the community in school improvement.

These appearances promote not only the product (the school), but also the leader. These experiences and relationships can benefit the leader through the trials and tribulations that true difference-makers often run into. School leaders committed to bringing about change will undoubtedly face adversity. When the most powerful people in a community believe in the mission and vision, believe in the product, and believe in the leader, the leader gains a larger margin for error.

The role of an educational leader can be compared to the fast-paced, 24-hour news cycle. Educators, like politicians and other headliners, cannot escape public scrutiny (Sterrett, 2011). At the gym. In the grocery store. At church. While pumping gas. At dinner. While playing with their children in the park. At the local bar. At a movie two towns over. At the game. Even in the public restroom! Everywhere, a school leader will be asked, "So, how is it going over there?"

Establishing a consistent, positive, and honest message can go an enormous way toward engaging community citizens in the improvement process of a school. Leaders who just respond "Good" to this perennial question do not serve the purpose of the school. It may serve the purpose of the leaders—in trying to get back to whatever they were doing, but it does not serve the school. Every principal needs a few different versions of a stump speech that will best satisfy the needs of the school: the 45-second speech, the two-minute speech, and the ten-minute speech.

♦ **The 45-second speech:** This is the most common speech that you will give. This speech is appropriate when asked the question in a place where movement is appropriate— for instance, in the movie theater lobby or in the checkout line at the grocery store. The 45-second speech should articulate the school vision and a school improvement goal or two: *"Things are going really well. We are not where we want to someday be—the best small school in the state, but we are working toward that goal. The kids and the staff are great. We are working real hard to get the kids out into the community this year—our number of completed service hours is way up since September."*

♦ **The two-minute speech:** This speech is appropriate when in a static position. The most common occasion for the two-minute speech is at a sporting event. The two-minute speech resembles the 45-second speech with the addition of a message about something new you want to promote that the community is or will ultimately be talking about. In addition to the above: *". . . We are very excited to be getting a new computer lab for next year. That is really going to help the improvement progress. Other than that, everything is going well, but it is going to be hard to move forward without Ken. He has worked in the building for more than 30 years, but nobody deserves to enjoy retirement more than he does."*

♦ **The ten-minute speech:** The ten-minute speech is the scariest and always the most impromptu. The ten-minute speech occurs when you are attending a Rotary meeting as a member and the guest speaker does not show. It occurs when you attend a school district board meeting because students are being recognized and you are asked to give an update on the status of the school. These occurrences are rare—and can be intimidating—but are always great opportunities to share the successes of the school. The ten-minute speech should be an engaging and inspiring verbal rendition of the school improvement plan. This allows the community to know the current status and future hopes of the school and then plan how to realize such goals.

Undoubtedly, an administrator is asked this question more often than other school personnel; however, others are also asked.

This underscores the significance of all members of the organization having a similar message. If the principal answers the question with "Everything is great" and the assistant principal discusses how difficult the year has been, credibility and trust diminish for both people and the school. *Highly effective school systems communicate with such precision that everybody from the superintendent to the evening janitor would be able to articulate major initiatives and desired outcomes.*

Spreading the Word

Schools are not businesses. Schools are not selling a product. Thus, promoting the activities of a school often becomes an afterthought or an activity that is mindlessly delegated by the principal. Even for those school leaders who focus on communication, it still remains hard to quantify the effectiveness of public relations activity because there is no financial bottom line to analyze. As a result, public relations can take an awful lot of time yet have little impact. This makes the task daunting; however, by systematizing the approach, school leaders can maximize the impact of their public relations efforts while not significantly adding to their workload.

There are two major vehicles for disseminating positive news about a school: the press and the people. A school must operate from the paradigm that positive press is to be sought and earned; it is not a right of a school. Too many school leaders are passive instead of proactively seeking to accommodate the media and disseminate information; they end up with an adversarial relationship because administration perceives that the only press about their school is negative or sensationalized. As a result, many new administrators fear or simply avoid the press and the limelight. In those situations, the principal must make a conscious choice to do whatever it takes to repair those relationships and move the image of a school forward.

The press is there to provide a service to the public, not to the schools. With that in mind, school leaders should seek out ways to accommodate the needs of the local press and thus promote their organizations. The needs and wants of each local entity are going to be vastly different, so each principal must build a relationship with the local media. Suggestions for creating such a relationship include the following:

- Set up a summer lunch meeting with the editor of each local press agency.
- Ask the editor what you can do to promote your school. Is there a timeline that you should operate under? Is there a standard press release format to use?
  - ◇ Local media may prefer the basic who-what-why-where-when-how press release, in which case they would want to receive raw information from the school before deciding if and how it will be reported.
  - ◇ Some media outlets prefer pre-prepared press releases that can be immediately embedded into a newscast or newspaper. If that is the case, take the time to craft stories to support the requests of your local media.
- Negotiate the cost of a monthly insert for your school.
- Follow requests from the local media. For instance, if the paper prefers to receive potential stories on Tuesdays, then send over the stories on Tuesdays. If your paper will only print stories accompanied by a picture, always provide a picture.

Operating in this manner will not cure all school/media relations, but it will be a start to mending broken fences if need be and will strengthen already friendly relations. After all, a principal cannot expect to improve a poor relationship with the press by simply doing nothing. Such a conversation can cause significant positive change in how a school communicates with the media. For instance, some schools send electronic copies of speeches to be given by school leaders (for example, at commencement, National Honor Society induction, or freshman orientation), allowing the media to pick out the key elements of the speech without the possibility of misquoting. This five-second task serves as a win-win; many more possibilities exist, but often go unknown because school leaders never take that first step in forging a relationship with all local media outlets.

Community Service

> *Even in the most affluent areas, the greatest resource of a school is its students.*

In times of crisis, no nation rallies like the United States. In desperate times, quite often schools are at the epicenter of relief efforts. Reports from the relief efforts after Hurricane Katrina in 2005 noted that the combined support received from schools exceeded that of any major corporation. More than $10 million was raised through bake sales and other community outreach programs organized by students and schools. This indicates what is possible for students and schools when there is a shared belief in a cause.

School leaders must engage their students in the community so that they learn to be the change they would like to see in their community. Almost every school mission statement notes that the fundamental purpose of a school is to assist students in becoming productive citizens. This outcome, however, is almost completely ignored in most school programming and systems. Very few schools have a commitment to teaching students about service and selfless contributions to society. Simply attaching a 10-, 20-, or even 40-hour community service requirement to graduation does not serve to enact the mission. A concentrated, focused effort needs to be made by all schools to foster a productive, responsible citizenry through the commitment to service—starting in the primary grades. This is a far-too-often forgotten-about 21st-century skill.

Here are some creative ways for principals to encourage service by their students:

- Designate quarterly service days.
- Make service a prerequisite for all clubs and activities (including sports).
- Give incentives for students to engage in service.
  - assemblies
  - graduation recognition
  - letters of recommendation
- Embed service opportunities into the curriculum.

- Seek out and promote opportunities (for example, create a service Facebook page or Twitter account).
- Use student service as a resource in the school or district (for example, supplying technology assistance and troubleshooting, tutoring students, reading to elementary or pre-K students).
- Use voluntary service as a way to offset discipline or even student fees.
- Seek out community partnerships.
- Create service opportunities in areas of student interest.
- Use service instead of "filler" on days with amended and distracting schedules.
- Bring service to the kids (quilt-making, Walk for the Cure, blood drives) by housing activities at the school.

Thinking "outside the box" is a common term that is too vague to have any impact. A better description of this activity is creating ideas or possibilities by extending yourself and others outside of your comfort zones. Leaders seldom do that with students. Time-consuming tasks that are valuable to a school, but a drain on personnel can often be used to extend curriculum and provide opportunities for students. The most common area where administrators have begun to view students as an asset is in the realm of technology. Many schools now provide a structured opportunity for students to use their advanced technical skills to repair networks, provide support for teachers, and troubleshoot everyday problems with the school's computer systems. This barely scratches the surface of service possibilities for students.

Creating independent study programs in small schools to allow students with talents that cannot be served by the traditional curriculum is an additional option. This past year, students at my high school worked through independent study programs to create a website detailing the history of the town and also worked to create videos that supported the mission and vision of the school, including an anti-bullying video that gained national recognition.

If one grade level of students donates one morning of time to their community once a month, that can quickly amount to more than 10,000 hours of service per year. Think of the impact! In one day students could accomplish so much—they could clean out school district or YMCA lockers and disinfect the locker room, paint murals, visit with special-needs adults in nursing homes, plant a garden at a residence for the elderly, clean up trash at a local river, and read to elementary school students. Such services not only provide invaluable public relations, but also can have a profound impact on local agencies by saving them thousands of dollars in man-hours.

School clubs and athletics are a privilege and not a right. School leaders should clearly articulate to sponsors, coaches, and students that a requirement of participation is community service. Such service will be a culture-changing activity for many schools, although it need not deter organizations from their original purpose. Often such service can be used as a team-building activity that serves the greater purpose of the team while supporting the community. For such an expectation to have maximum impact, the students' action should be noted and rewarded. Hanging banners in the gym noting the number of hours of service that the team has contributed as well as an overall GPA will draw considerable attention from the parents of the school community—and from visitors. Celebrate successes in service. Leaders must remember that what is important and valuable to a school and community is transparent, discussed, and rewarded when done well.

Call to Action: Lead Change

If you are walking down the right path and you're willing to keep walking, eventually you will make progress.

—*President Barack Obama*

I love America. I love the American way of educating students. I sincerely believe that the way our students are educated plays a major role in why they generally emerge as the most innovative, socially adept, and socially aware people on the planet. Being proud of what we do as educators, however, must be very different from being content with the current performance. Change needs to occur. The American way of educating students today must not be the way we educate students in 2020, let alone 2040.

This book was designed to tell school leaders throughout the country that there simply is no easy way out. There is no prepackaged curriculum, RtI model, discipline program, or comprehensive improvement model that will fix all that ails American schools. We must be the change we want to see in our schools, in our society, and in our country.

Leading change is an extraordinarily difficult and complex task. Having a mind-set of service and support allows a leader to facilitate this process in a consistent and focused manner. Working to enact your school's mission, to support the professionals in your building, to serve the needs of your students, and to provide the type of school your community deserves should drive everything you do every day. Start there. Start at the core. Start with yourself—and begin leading change today.

REFERENCES

Ainsworth, L. (2011). *Rigorous curriculum design: How to create curricular units of study that align standards, instruction, and assessment.* Lanham, MD: Advanced Learning Press.

Altoona Area School District. (n.d.). *Vision and values statements.* Retrieved May 15, 2012, from http://qsite.aasdcat.com/vision_values_statements.htm.

Barber, M., & Mourshed, M. (2007). *How the world's best-performing schools come out on top.* McKinsey & Company.

Berra, Y. (n.d.). Retrieved August 23, 2012, from http://thinkexist.com/quotation/you-ve_got_to_be_very_careful_if_you_don-t_know/150217.html.

Brophy, J. (1976). *Motivating students to learn.* Boston: McGraw-Hill.

Brown, J. L., & Moffett, C. A. (1999). *The hero's journey: How educators can transform schools and improve learning.* Alexandria, VA: ASCD.

Curwin, R. L., & Mendler, A. N. (1988). *Discipline with dignity.* Alexandria, VA: ASCD.

Danielson, C. (1996). *Enhanced professional practice: A framework for teaching.* Alexandria, VA: ASCD.

Danielson, C. (2011). *The framework for teacher evaluation instrument.* Princeton: The Danielson Group.

Deal, T. E., & Peterson, K. D. (1999). *Shaping school culture: The heart of leadership.* San Francisco: Jossey-Bass.

Dean, C. B., Hubbell, E. R., Pitler, H., & Stone, B. (2012). *Classroom instruction that works: Research-based strategies for increasing student achievement* (2nd ed.). Alexandria, VA: ASCD.

Dillon, S. (2010). *Top scores from Shanghai stun educators.* Retrieved May 30, 2012, from http://www.nytimes.com/2010/12/07/education/07education.html?pagewanted=all.

Dodson, F. (n.d.). Retrieved August 23, 2012, from http://www.quotecollection.com/quote/goals-that-are-not-written-down-are-just-wishes/.

DuFour, R. (2006). Foreword. *Transforming school culture.* Bloomington, IN: Solution Tree.

Elmore, R. (2002). *Bridging the gap between standards and achievement: The imperative for professional development in education.* Washington DC: Albert Shanker Institute.

Freiberg H. J. (1993). A school that fosters resilience in inner-city youth. *Journal of Negro Education, 62*(3), 364. Retrieved February 12, 2012, from http://www.jstor.org/pss/2295471.

Glatthorn, A. A. (2000). *The principal as curriculum leader: Shaping what is taught and tested* (2nd ed.). Thousand Oaks, CA: Corwin Press.

Grandin, T. (n.d.). Retrieved August 23, 2012, from http://www.brainyquote.com/quotes/authors/t/temple_grandin.html.

Hebert, E. A. (2006). *The boss of the whole school.* New York: Teachers College Press.

Heckscher, C. (1994). Defining the post-bureaucratic type. In A. Donnellon, & C. Heckscher, *The post-bureaucratic organization: New perspectives on organizational change* (p. 14). Thousand Oaks, CA: Sage Publications.

Himmele, P., & Himmele, W. (2011). *Total participation techniques: Making every student an active learner.* Alexandria, VA: ASCD.

Jensen, E. (2009). *Teaching with poverty in mind*. Alexandria, VA: ASCD.

Kennedy Middle School. (n.d.). *Mission and vision*. Retrieved May 19, 2012, http://kennedy.psjaisd.us/apps/pages/index. jsp?uREC_ID=120687&type=d&pREC_ID=259160&hide Menu=1.

Laertius, D. (n.d.). Retrieved August 23, 2012, from http://www.quotationspage.com/quote/29267.html.

Lincoln, A. (n.d.). Retrieved August 23, 2012, from http://www.brainyquote.com/quotes/quotes/a/abrahamlin133687.html.

Lumpa, D., & Whitaker, T. (2005). *Great quotes for great educators*. Larchmont, NY: Eye On Education.

Maiers, A., & Sandvold, A. (2011). *The passion-driven classroom: A framework for teaching and learning*. Larchmont, NY: Eye On Education.

Maslow, A. (1943). A theory of human motivation, *Psychological Review, 50*(4), 370–396.

Martin Luther King High School. (n.d.). *Martin Luther King High School 2011–2012 student/parent handbook*. Retrieved May 25, 2012, from http://rusd.schoolwires.net/cms/lib3/CA01001728/Centricity/Domain/46/PDF%20Files/StudentHandbook2011.pdf.

Mayo, T. (Winter 2010). The importance of vision. *Harvard Business Review OnPoint*, 8.

Muhammed, A. (2009). *Transforming school culture: How to overcome staff division*. Bloomington, IN: Solution Tree.

Nightingale, E. (n.d.). Retrieved August 23, 2012, from http://thinkexist.com/quotation/our_environment-the_world_in_which_we_live_and/323373.html.

Obama, B. (n.d.). Retrieved August 23, 2012, from http://www.goodreads.com/quotes/31655-if-you-re-walking-down-the-right-path-and-you-re-willing.

Overbaugh, R. C., & Schultz, L. (n.d.). *Bloom's taxonomy*. Old Dominion University. Retrieved July 29, 2012, from http://www.odu.edu/educ/roverbau/Bloom/blooms_taxonomy.htm.

Palahniuk, C. (n.d.). Retrieved August 23, 2012, from http://thinkexist.com/quotation/the-trick-to-forgetting-the-big-picture-is-to/365778.html.

Pink, D. (2009). *Drive*. New York: Riverhead Books.

Popham, J. (2003). *Test better, teach better: The instructional role of assessment*. Alexandria, VA: ASCD.

Popham, J. (2008). *Transformative assessment*. Alexandria, VA: ASCD.

Porsche, F. (n.d.). Retrieved August 23, 2012, from http://www.brainyquote.com/quotes/quotes/f/ferdinandp304803.html

Ramis, H. (n.d.). Retrieved August 23, 2012, from http://www.goodquotes.com/quote/harold-ramis/nothing-reinforces-a-professional-rela.

Reeves, D. (2006). *The learning leader: How to focus school improvement for better results*. Alexandria, VA: ASCD.

Shaw, G. B. (n.d.). Retrieved August 23, 2012, from http://thinkexist.com/quotation/the_single_biggest_problem_in_communication_is/155222.html.

Sterrett, W. (2011). *Insights into action*. Alexandria, VA: ASCD.

Stewart, V. (2012). *A world-class education: Learning from international models of excellence and innovation*. Alexandria, VA: ASCD.

University High School. (n.d.). *University High School: Course catalog 2011–2012*. Retrieved May 15, 2012, from http://www.iusd.org/UHS/Academics/documents/UHSCourseCatalog201112.pdf.

Wilson, J. (2008, April 23). Retrieved August 23, 2012, from http://www.forbes.com/2008/04/23/imagine-cup-winners-oped-cx_jwi_0423imagine.html.